D1799778

Peace, War, and Mental Health: Couples Therapists Look at the Dynamics

Peace, War, and Mental Health: Couples Therapists Look at the Dynamics

Barbara Jo Brothers
Editor

The Haworth Press, Inc.
New York • London • Norwood (Australia)

Peace, War, and Mental Health: Couples Therapists Look at the Dynamics has also been published as *Journal of Couples Therapy*, Volume 3, Number 4 1992.

The Haworth Press, Inc., 10 Alice Street, Binghamton, NY 13904-1580, USA

Library of Congress Cataloging-in-Publication Data

Peace, war, and mental health : couples therapists look at the dynamics / Barbara Jo Brothers, editor.
    p. cm.
    "Has also been published as Journal of couples therapy, v. 3, no. 4, 1992"-Copr. p.
    Includes bibliographical references.
    ISBN 1-56024-437-2
    1. Marital psychotherapy. 2. Interpersonal conflict. 3. War-Psychological aspects. 4. Persian Gulf War, 1991-Psychological aspects. I. Brothers, Barbara, 1940- .
RC488.5.P39 1993
616.89'156-dc20   93-18004
                                                                                     CIP

Peace, War, and Mental Health: Couples Therapists Look at the Dynamics

CONTENTS

ABOUT THE EDITOR

Barbara Jo Brothers, MSW, BCD, a Diplomate in Clinical Social Work, National Association of Social Workers, is in private practice in New Orleans. She received her BA from the University of Texas and her MSW from Tulane University, where she is currently on the faculty. She was editor of *The Newsletter of the American Academy of Psychotherapists* from 1976 to 1985, and was Associate Editor of *Voices: The Art and Science of Psychotherapy* from 1979 to 1989. She has nearly 30 years of experience, in both the public and private sectors, helping people to form skills that will enable them to connect emotionally. The author of numerous articles and book chapters on authenticity in human relating, she has advocated healthy, congruent communication that builds intimacy as opposed to destructive, incongruent communication which blocks intimacy. In addition to her many years of direct work with couples and families, Ms. Brothers had led numerous workshops on teaching communication in families and has also played an integral role in the development of training programs in family therapy for mental health workers throughout the Louisiana state mental health system. She is a board member of the Institute for International Connections, a non-profit organization for cross-cultural professional development, focused on training and cross-cultural exchange with psychotherapists in Russia, republics once part of what used to be the Soviet Union, and other Eastern European countries.

Make Love Not War–
Or at Least Make Meaning

Barbara Jo Brothers

This volume was born of my outrage about the outbreak of the Persian Gulf War in the Winter of 1991, which I expressed in "Ask Not For Whom The Siren Wails"(Brothers, 1991b), and out of the subsequent hope engendered in me by the outbreak of *peace* suggested in victory of the people in the failed coup in Russia in the summer of 1991, "Hope for Healing in Russia: Reflections and Epilogue" (Brothers, 1992).

What do outbreaks of wars and outbreaks of peace have to do with couples therapy? That question is at least addressed, if not answered, in the following collection of articles.

The interview with Virginia Satir by Sheldon Starr provides rationale for this theme of linking war among nations to war between couples. Virginia's position is that prevention may be expanded to include the "mental health" of the whole world; her corollary position that change is possible through engagement of the passion of only a small percentage of the population certainly proved true in Moscow in August 1991.

Zur and Glendinning speak to "the role of gender on warmaking and its potential impact on peace-making," taking a systems approach to examining that relationship between the two. Shub takes a less-than-optimistic stance that the once apparently deep flow of the humanistic movement has somehow soaked soundlessly into the sands of time: we have failed to bring into popular awareness the importance and implications of humanistic values. Golden makes the bridge between domestic violence and large scale violence as lying in societal attitudes. Expert in domestic violence, she points to a shift in attitude as the critical factor in saving us from self-destruc-

1

tion, making a persuasive case for the role community has in tolerating violence within families and between nations.

Natural-born citizen of South Africa and voluntary exile living in London, Petruska Clarkson makes the link between the potential for resolution of differences in couples and in nations showing the similar characteristics through a thorough discussion of dealing with difference.

Margaret Kirschner's focus on our longing for belonging as paradoxical in the face of our all being part of a Whole: "We must love others as ourselves because, in fact, others *are* ourselves" and believes psychology is incomplete without spirituality. Alma Silverthorn takes exception to a desire to pool psychology with spirituality, with wry warning about the propensity of our psychological professions to try to force everything into a test tube and a category.

Forming a kind of ballast to the images of light from Kirschner, Felder informs us with radical honesty by means of her own fascination with—and indulgence in—malice. Providing the shadow for Kirschner's light and brightness, she goes, like one knowing the path, straight to the heart of the destructive war dynamic: *"The exhilaration of victory (seeing the pain embodied in an 'other') masks the aches within our own nation's soul."* Felder is an ordained minister. Perhaps she provides some comfort to the concern raised by Silverthorn about an unholy marriage between psychology and spirituality. Would that we all might be able to be so open and honest about our own flirtations with evil. Evil *owned* is evil contained. And were we to stay honest to our humanity, we would not find ourselves bound in the pages of a DSMIII of the spiritual.

Tom Greening's beautifully bitter poem on the carnage of the Persian Gulf war lies between the Kirschner and Felder articles, his imagery burning the scenes back into our memories.

Atwood and Maltin present the major tasks of relationship building along with the traps that mitigate against good relationships forming. Dreyfus and the Becvars present nuts and bolts articles in the how of conflict resolution between the pair, the one on application and the other on theory.

Cupp speaks both personally and clinically to the issue of warring versus loving, pointing out how the former is served by either/or thinking.

Dreyfus has developed some very real tools to effect conflict intervention for real life–and done so in a gorgeously concrete detail: she has developed a set of flash cards which facilitate each member of the pair in *presenting his or her real feelings underneath the guard that goes with conflict.* The invention of the flashcards was her way of producing an effective method of "throwing a little decency" into the middle of the fray and "to find out that being genuine 'works,' that one's own realness is inherently friendly, connective and peace-producing (and not alienating, as often feared) is a cornerstone of good couples work." With her flash-cards, Dreyfus tangibly creates a way to "make meaning" and, therefore, enable the couple to move out of a war zone and to a context where peace is possible.

Giving case examples, the Becvars show their use of a systems perspective, how they operate out of an epistemology of participation as opposing one of placing blame. In their comment on Becvars' article, Sam and Diana Kirschner make the case that, while a systems perspective is useful, it is not, in their experience, enough. They bring up the importance of also discovering and understanding the individual dynamics of each of the two partners.

Wars start with alienation between people. Peace starts with the connection of hearts. The former may be seen as issuing from patterns that *dis*connect (to paraphrase Gregory Bateson, 1979, p. 8) while the latter is a feature of the Pattern that Connects (to paraphrase Jean Houston, 1987, paraphrasing Gregory Bateson). There is a relationship–a correlation–between functional or dysfunctional communication, peace versus war, and the esteem in which one holds oneself and others (Brothers, 1990, 1991a). I understand that John Bradshaw says 95% of families are dysfunctional; he is paraphrasing Virginia Satir. What she actually said: "Only about 5% of the time do families engage in the kind of congruent communication that will build bridges rather than walls" (Virginia Satir. Personal Communication. August, 1971). From that observation, I drew the concept, "Make Love Not War–Or, at Least Make Meaning": Build bridges, not walls–and reach an open hand across any remaining abyss. Struggle to find out what the other is *really* feeling/thinking/needing underneath whatever defensive wrapping.

The Gulf War "built" a fiery chasm, proving technology now makes it possible to throw up such walls with blinding speed and accuracy. The Event in Moscow bridged a moat, alive with 50 years worth of snapping, snarling and waiting nuclear warheads–proving those bridges *can* be built over even the worst of pits.

As fast as this world is moving, some other international events of appalling or inspiring nature may have taken place by the time this volume comes off the presses, moving the minds of the American public away from these two contrasting events in 1991. However, as psychotherapist, I believe it is our role to reflect on psychohistory as an extension of systems thinking and to point to ways human interaction can be seen to be related in the macrosystems as well as in the microsystems. It is also the role of the psychotherapist to empower the client/patient to move beyond the archaic defenses learned in childhood; Homo sapiens have a much wider choice in behavior than the narrow "flight or fight" used by mammals with less complex brains.

I am reminded of Sergei, who drove to work right through the middle of Moscow on the second day of the coup past all the rows of tanks–with the small red, blue and white flag of the republic of Russia flying from his radio antenna. He had sat up the night before and made it himself. I am reminded of 25 year old Olga, who grabbed the soldier's arm, preventing him from ripping the underground news bulletin off the subway wall until she had finished reading it. They neither fought nor flew. They simply made what they thought and wanted abundantly clear–even in the face of loaded guns, armed troops.

In the segment of the interview with Virginia Satir that follows in this volume, she extends the mental health concept of prevention, referring to her calculations that a change in only 20% of the world's population could push us over edges toward peace:

> Statistically, if 20% of the world is into a new place we've made it . . . Because that is all it takes to get a new thing going. *Twenty percent of the population. Six percent to start it off and then another fourteen percent to make it go.* Those are the movers and shakers in the world. And if we can get that many we'll have it, we can do it. . . . it is also one of the other reasons

why, for me, any therapeutic transaction that decreases a person's self-esteem, demeans or humiliates them defeats the purpose of making this a better world.

I was struck with the echo of Virginia's calculations in the following statement in Hedrick Smith's *The New Russians,* written just prior to the attempted coup in the summer of 1991.

" . . . The big surprise for Gorbachev is that there was such a grass-roots upheaval," commented Boris Kurashvili, a scholar at the Institute of State and Law and a daring exponent of reform under Brezhnev. "There will be independent, unmanageable deputies in the new People's Congress–I figure *twenty percent.*"
"*Ten percent* is enough to have an opposition that can be heard," Kurashvili emphasized. "There will be enough to form an opposition, an independent bloc." [Italics mine]
(Smith, 1990, p. 451)

Once I was walking with a friend along a beach on one of the cays off the coast of Belize. A group of at least ten men were trying to turn over the helm of a very large boat–to paint it or something like that. Red in the face and dripping with perspiration from the weight of the unyielding boat, they motioned to my friend (size 12, *may*be 125 pounds) and me to come help. We put our shoulders to the hull along side the swarthy, muscular, surf-built islanders, adding the amount of heave the pair of us had to offer–such as it was.

And the boat lifted and turned over.

And the coup lifted and the government turned over.

And the world would "lift" and we could stand up for what we need without shooting each other as we rise.

Many people behave as though they have only got two possibilities, to attack . . . or capitulate. Those are two you can use, but you can also do something quite different.

–Virginia Satir, 1985

REFERENCES

Bateson, G. (1979). Mind in nature. New York: E.P. Dutton.

Brothers, B.J. (1990). Intimacy and autonomy: connecting. *Journal of Couples Therapy, 1,* 3/4, 1-8.

Brothers, B.J. (1991a). Methods for connectedness: Virginia Satir's contribution to the process of human communication. *Journal of Couples Therapy, 2,* 1/2, 11-20.

Brothers, B.J. (1991b). Ask not for whom the siren wails. *Journal of Couples Therapy, 2,* 3, 11-16.

Brothers, B.J. (1992). Hope for healing in Russia: reflections and epilogue. *Journal of Couples Therapy, 3,* 2/3.

Houston, J. (1987). The search for the beloved. Los Angeles: Jeremy P. Tarcher.

Satir, V. *Speaker.* (1985). An Interview with Virginia Satir by Sheldon Starr, PhD. (Available from Sheldon Starr, PhD, 801 Welch Road, #209, Palo Alto, CA 94304).

Smith, H. (1990). *The new Russians.* New York: Random House.

Prevention:
Changing Our Whole Culture–
An Interview with Virginia Satir:

Sheldon Starr

After I learn to see a family, I see a microcosm of the whole world because the family is a microcosm of a whole world . . .
–Virginia Satir

[Early in 1985 I asked Virginia Satir if she was willing to be interviewed on videotape concerning her thinking about family therapy at that time and especially with regard to any ideas she might wish to share with the family therapy community. The interview took place on March 15, 1985 at Virginia's home in Menlo Park, California. The transcript of the interview is 60 pages, and this is the fifth of a series of segments from that interview covering different themes.[1]]

STARR: Okay, but we are not talking about Family Therapy now, rather we are talking about anything therapeutic.

Sheldon Starr, PhD, was founder and director for 15 years of the Family Study Unit, a family therapy training and treatment program at the V.A. Medical Center, Palo Alto, CA when this interview was conducted. Dr. Starr is presently Professor of Psychology (part time) at Pacific Graduate School of Psychology and is in private practice, both in Palo Alto, CA. His association with Virginia Satir spanned 25 years, first as student, then as associate and long-time friend. Correspondence may be addressed to 801 Welch Road, #209, Palo Alto, CA 94304.

1. A highly condensed and edited summary of the entire interview appeared in the AFTA Newsletter, Fall 1985 and that version consisted of less than 20% of the interview.

[The use of brackets [ ] and italics are editorial additions for the purpose of clarity and/or emphasis.] S.S.

SATIR: Alright, let me tell you something. Everything that is good therapeutically is good for the family. What the family enables us to do is that the seeds of how the problem arose carry the opportunity for how the family can be healed. Those of us who worked with individuals always had the family in [our mental] background. When you remember that everyone is born little, you have to think about the parents. So that when you switched to Family Therapy what you added was all of the interactions that influence the human being and we have a first hand opportunity to change these. The reason for working with the whole family is that you have the chance to do something much more creative, to heal in a much more effective way. You have the opportunity to intervene so that other family members do not have to continue in some kind of . . .

STARR: It's really doing some kind of preventive work.

SATIR: Absolutely! For me it is *preventive and educational.* After I get to know a family I see a microcosm of the whole world because the family is a microcosm of the whole world.

STARR: A family is where you learn to make it in this world.

SATIR: Well yes, and we look around at our public, international relations, and what do we have? We have the United States and Russia who are a married couple who do not live together. They [in turn] have a very strong oldest son—nobody knows who the mother is—that is China. Then they have a whole lot of so-called kids, the Western nations like France, Germany, etc. Then there are the kids who come from the other side of the tracks, probably illegitimate in their [U.S. and Russia] minds, mainly the Third World countries.

STARR: Fine, that's great. Suppose we pursue that. How do we use family concepts to avert nuclear disaster? Because that is implied in what we are talking about.

SATIR: Yup. I think about this a great deal. The first thing for me is to do and be all I can to shed light, to help people open up and to enable us to develop the kind of consciousness that makes it possible for us to join and cooperate [= collaborate]. Cooperation is the first thing, *number one*; if we do not do that, nothing else matters. On one level that's a big job.

STARR: Oh yes, but it's easier to talk about than to do it.

SATIR: I belong to [many] peace groups and I find that one of the most important functions that I fulfill is to help [people] to be cooperative [collaborative]. To [collaborate] is such an alien idea to us [Western civilization], that it requires a huge amount of energy to deal with. I would predict that if we were able–you and Joan Herrick and everybody else that we know were able to consciously handle ourselves in such a way as to *reflect the light that we have in our being* and [do so] in our dealings with people, that [alien idea] would move. And there are people moving [reflecting the light] already. What we need is to [increase that movement]; then we speak with an [amplified] voice. The creative energy will change what is going on. But the place where everyone can behave in this *new way*, so to speak, [lies] in the *development* of their own consciousness, in the work they do, in the workplace, in the therapy office, in the schools. Alright. Now I believe that and I see it [happening] because people learn how they can connect with somebody else.

STARR: But now you are talking about changing our whole culture.

SATIR: That's right, and that is what has to happen.

STARR: What bothers me [about this] is that there are some things that are happening that fly in the face of whether people are actually changing in the direction of collaboration. I am thinking about the escalation of violence and the increase in child abuse, just to name two issues.

SATIR: Alright. Okay.

STARR: What we are talking about is: "Hey, you know, we are not making it." We are not headed in the right direction right now. If you survey what is happening, you do not feel that we are doing what you are suggesting we must do.

SATIR: Well, you see at what point do we decide we've gone to the wall? At what point do we decide that we [*must*] change? Is it going to be when we kill each other, everybody?

STARR: It looks like that sometimes, doesn't it? That's what is so scary. Is that what has to happen? Must we have a nuclear war somewhere?

SATIR: Alright. Okay. Let me tell you what I think about that. First, there are [approximately] 4.5 billion people on the face of this earth [in 1985]. There is no way you or I are going to connect with these people.

STARR: For sure.

SATIR: Alright, I know that. I was depressed until I figured out that I couldn't do it. We're talking about *changing* [to develop an international social structure based on collaboration which would result in preserving this planet]. I have already mentioned the first way to change. It starts with me, it doesn't start with you or me starting with you. [We are each individually responsible.] Then we need to start [changing] our institutions, and much is already beginning to change in the workplace. A great many humanistic things are going on in the workplace that have to do with helping people to work more collaboratively. Then a great deal is beginning to happen in our schools, like the development of educational networks which is getting a lot of support, [and a greater sensitivity to developing self-esteem]. When we look at [positive] changes in the workplace and schools and compare these with fifty years ago, there is no comparison, none whatsoever! People can now get together in groups and what they need to learn is how to *be* together so that they can make something happen [change]. You know, actually all the trouble made by people we hear about–child and spouse abuse and drug addiction and all–probably does not touch more than 10% of our population. But the impact is so great that it looks bad.

STARR: That comes to a lot more people than family therapists see. You're talking about 20 million people.

SATIR: Of course. Family therapists can also do something about influencing people. I happen now to be into something on aggression and violence and I'm into more peace groups where I am doing whatever I can do. I figured out that my most important [function] is to help people connect and to develop morals [a perspective or world view that favors human beings] about how they can collaborate together. *We all have to do this!* Nobody can do it alone and there is no concept that's going to make it. We have to do it, and I think what we have to face is that each of us has to be a part of all this [shift in values that would also facilitate a world movement to collaborate for peace]. Statistically, if 20% of the world is into a new place, we've made it!

STARR: How so?

SATIR: Because all it takes to get a new thing [social structure or social order] going is 20% of the population. [All you need is] 6% to start it off and then another 14% to make it go.[1] These are the movers and shakers in the world. And if we can get that many we can do it. And that's the only thing that makes me feel alright about going on. It's because I know there are a lot of other [dedicated] people; I meet them every day. It's also one of the other reasons why for me, any therapeutic transaction that decreases a person's self-esteem, demeans or humiliates them, defeats the purpose of making this a better world.

STARR: Sure, who would disagree with you?

SATIR: Oh [hesitatingly]. I . . .

STARR: You think people would disagree with that?

SATIR: When I say it like that, no, but when I point out what people are doing and that is what it is, they don't act like it.

STARR: Okay, they don't act like it.

NOTE

1. Ms. Satir on other occasions had focused attention on the downside of bringing about changes in society, by indicating that Adolf Hitler may have initially had smaller numbers to bring about his social order because of his tactics. Indeed, Ms. Satir was well aware of the frightening possibilities inherent in the relatively small percentage of population needed to *instigate* significant social change.

Perhaps not captured in the transcript of this interview, was Ms. Satir's contagious optimism about changing our social structure from competitive to collaborative, from alienated to connected, and from hateful and violent to loving and peaceful. Her optimism about change invaded her clinical work, always in my opinion, to the benefit of her clients. Although to my knowledge she did not predict the changes which have taken place in Europe since her death, were she still alive I could envision her knowingly nodding and saying, "Well, of course . . . ."

Men/Women, War/Peace:
A Systems Approach

Chellis Glendinning
Ofer Zur

[Editor's Note: Although "Men/Women, War/Peace: A Systems Approach" was originally published only five years prior to its appearance in the Journal of Couples Therapy, there have been major occurrences in world affairs in that amount of time that have resulted in some changes. For example, the article alludes to women having been traditionally excluded from the military. Unfortunately or fortunately, depending upon one's point of view, women do now "go to war": the Persian Gulf War provided that "career-building equal opportunity." However, the traditional of view of women as not having a warrior role can still be considered to exist in our culture, broadly speaking. The basic thrust of the article would seem to remain true.]

"Baby is born!" This was the cable the Manhattan Project sent to President Truman to report the first atom bomb test.

- The revealing Bikini bathing suit was named for the Pacific islands where nuclear testing took place.

Chellis Glendinning, PhD, is a psychologist, lecturer, and workshop facilitator. She is a director at ecological think-tank, the Elmwood Institute, in Berkeley, CA. She is the author of the Pulitzer Prize-nominated *When Technology Wounds* (Morrow) and of *Waking Up in the Nuclear Age* (New Society). She is currently working on a book about addiction and the ecological crisis. Correspondence may be addressed to Box 381 Tesuque, NM 87574.

This article was published as Chapter 10 in *Solutions for a Troubled World*, edited by Mark Macy, and is reprinted with permission by Earthview Press.

- We say: "All's fair in love and war.'
- Men tell "war stories" about their "conquests over" women.
- Connections between gender and war-making lie deep within the modern psyche.

Most of us are acquainted with the age-old battle between the sexes, which is based on a perception of rigid polarization of women and men. This polarization is also the main quality defining warfare.

While in everyday life men and women are split off from each other and from crucial aspects of themselves, war is the ultimate splitting of human from human. War also separates the population along sex lines, and in that respect it resembles childbirth. In war, women are additionally excluded from the military; in birthing, men were until recently excluded from the birthrooms. Also, to make nuclear war possible, our society splits the most fundamental material of existence–the atom–and so, as Albert Einstein predicted, "we drift toward unparalleled catastrophe." The nuclear threat brings urgency to the way we view warmaking, and the double-edged pain of sexism brings urgency to the way we view women and men. For survival, healing the splits is required (Glendinning, 1987).

The authors of this article bring humility to this task. We also bring hope. Our subject is the role of gender in warmaking and its potential impact on peacemaking. It is how, in the Nuclear Age, women and men can become participants in rites of passage towards the creation of more whole human beings and a more whole world order. As psychologists interested in social change, we take a systems approach. We attempt to understand our subject by identifying its many facets, their interrelationships, and the totality they form.

A FALSE BELIEF: MEN FIGHT, WOMEN LOVE

To begin, if we look at observable actions and interactions of men and women, we see that in wartime men are mobilized toward the front line and perceived as the warriors, aggressors and protectors. Women stay home. They are seen as the peace-loving, the passive, the protected. Consistent with this split is a myth, or collectively held belief, that war is a male institution that holds no appeal to women. Men assume the role of "the warrior," while to women falls the role of "the beautiful soul" (Zur, 1985).

Myths, as portrayed in literature, film, fairy tales, science, and everyday language and imagery, compel respect not necessarily for their truth, but because those who believe in them need them. Myths lay the basis for a society's perception of itself and its members' sense of identity. They also reflect a set of attitudes that, in the words of Joseph Campbell (1980), are "behavior perpetuators." Myths about war perpetuate warfare and as such, merit our special attention, especially in the face of nuclear holocaust (Harman, 1984; Zur, 1986A). Myths that men favor war while women are inherently peaceful reflect a dangerous and, as the reader will see, untrue split that keeps us from addressing the issues of gender imbalance and warfare with a fuller understanding.

It was personal experience that inspired Zur's research on aspects of the relationship between men, women and war. From a recent paper:

> In the 1973 War in the Middle East I served as a Lieutenant in a trained paratroopers' unit. We were kept at the rear, far from action, for the first part of the war. To my surprise, I found that most of the seasoned paratroopers in my unit devised any possible strategy to secure service at the front. When I questioned their motives, I discovered that their desire to return home to their wives and sweethearts with a glorious or grisly war story outweighed the fear of injury and high probability of death. I realized the incredible power of the women waiting at home on the soldiers at the front. Ultimately, it became obvious to me that the noncombatants, the protected, are an invisible but potent force at the front. (Zur, 1989)

A similar systems approach has been used by psychologists who study and intervene in cases of girls sexually abused by their fathers. Aggressor, victim and passive bystander each play a part. Without assigning blame to the girl-victim or the mother-bystander, diffusing responsibility of the abuser or denying the hierarchical power structure of the family, these therapists also explore the role of the mother who keeps her passive position, often denying reality for years.

When this systems approach is carried over to the context of war, we see that the role of the protector does not exist in a vacuum. A protector implies a protected person, and both of them rely on real and/or projected threats from the outside for role definition and identity formation (Stiehm, 1982).

In the case of nations, the protector is the military, an institution from which women are traditionally excluded. Men in political positions are the ones who usually define threats to the nation, who may in their own perceived interest exaggerate its potency, and whose exaggeration may provoke additional threats, further endangering both themselves and their protectees. Also, those who are protected often use the threat to test the protector and to enhance a real sense of personal safety.

BOYS PLAY TO WIN, GIRLS PLAY TO PLAY

The relationship among men, warriorship and war is complex. Regardless of innate differences between males and females, boys are socialized differently from girls. Qualities like assertiveness, courage to take physical risks, aggressiveness and lack of demonstrated emotions are encouraged so that men are set up to become "all they can be"–soldiers.

Differences are also initiated at a level deeper than socialization. Recent works by Nancy Chodorow (1978), Carol Gilligan (1982) and Dorothy Dinnerstein (1976) suggest that child-rearing structures in our culture produce differing perceptions of survival in male and female children–and therefore differing personalities. These theories stress the impact of nuclear families wherein mothers are the primary caretakers and fathers the primary breadwinners, unavailable emotionally or physically to the child.

According to Chodorow's theory, in order to develop a healthy gender identity, the male child must make a dramatic break with his primary love object and the person he depends on for physical and psychological survival–the mother. The problem begins when no adult male is present on a daily basis to turn to. Male development, then, is based on rejection of the female and everything associated with her, and then striving to relate to and identify with a distant, separate figure who lives in a world of rationality and rules (Chodorow, 1978).

In her studies of male and female moral development Gilligan (1982) demonstrates these same insights from the point of view of social perception. In this culture a male's sense of morality is based on impersonal and hierarchical definitions of what is right, and these are identified as the correct and most highly evolved ones.

Boys' games further illuminate this development. Games like basketball, football, racing and poker emphasize competing to win–to separate oneself out–and competing within the boundaries of set rules. If the rules don't succeed at containing the game, change the rules. If changes can't be negotiated or don't work, win by might.

Unlike boys, girls do not have to rupture with the primary love object and caretaker in order to develop a healthy gender identity. They can maintain the bond with Mother throughout their lives. A female sense of personal survival, then, is based on connection, relationship and communication. Women grow to have a fluid sense of boundaries and develop a relational sense of self. No attempt is made to separate oneself out, individuate or establish ego boundaries (Chodorow, 1978).

Gilligan carries these insights into the social realm. She finds that when judged by accepted male standards of moral development, females score "deficient." Yet she shows that females are indeed not deficient, but rather live by a different sense of morality. Women of all ages and backgrounds live in a world of relationship and social relativity, a world where awareness of the connection between people gives rise to a sense of responsibility for one another; where belief in communication is the primary mode of conflict resolution (Gilligan, 1982).

Lawrence Kohlberg (1969) observes that traditional girls' games like hopscotch, jump rope and jacks are turn-taking games in which competition is indirect and one person's winning does not depend on another's losing. Plus, when a quarrel breaks out–and, says Glendinning, I remember this from my childhood–girls tend to end the game rather than battle it out. As Gilligan (1982) claims, they subordinate "the continuation of the game to the continuation of the relationship."

WOMEN'S ROLE IN WARMAKING:
SUPPORTERS AND VICTIMS

Unlike the role of men during war, which is clear and apparent, the full role of women has not always been acknowledged. While men are at the front line, women are the protected at home, but they are also the soldiers at the home front. They are the Rosie-the-Riveters working in wartime industry; the Florence Nightingales healing the wounded; the worried mothers, proud sweethearts and acclaimed widows. They take care of all other noncombatants, and they participate in many operations of defense. Fulfilling these roles is an inherent and necessary part of the war effort. It is what enables the soldiers to carry out their complementary roles.

In recent research Zur and Morrison (1989) revealed that indeed women support warmaking, but for different reasons than men. While men favor war for abstract reasons—for defense of "freedom" and to protect allies with whom one has formal treaties—women support war when an appeal is made based on empathy for oppressed and vulnerable human beings. They also relate more easily to the dynamics of group cohesion and intensification of community during war as it is consistent with their psychological makeup. For example, women responded more favorably than men to such Likert-type items as:

- Aiding an attacked ally justifies war.
- One of the benefits of war is that it intensifies connections among civilians.
- Any country that violates the rights of innocent children should be invaded.

One of Zur's conclusions: women are not just the passive "beautiful souls" our myths describe them to be. They participate in war activities in numerous capacities, and they cooperate, support warmaking, and collude in it, albeit in different ways and for different reasons than men.

Women's relationship to war, however, is more complex. They are also its victims. On the other side of the proud mothers and enthusiastic workers lie the women who, as a class, never make the actual decision to wage war, but whose loss of father, husband, brother, son and lover always means devastating personal grief. For many women, this loss of relation and loved one also spells economic hardship for the rest of their lives. Second, women are the target of dehumanization in wartime pornography. Degrading pin-ups that reduce women to sexual objects are the constant companion of the troops in their barracks, planes and submarines. Dancing, singing women entertain soldiers at the front. Third, the vicious and violent rape of women is a universal and accepted part of men's violence in warring (Brownmiller, 1976). Finally, women are the victims of modern warfare in that the battlefields, which used to be far from the kitchens and marketplaces of society, are now anywhere that a long-range missile and its nuclear warhead can reach. Today all the world, and all the human beings in it, are the battlefield too.

The question then arises: How can women be both active supporters—nurses, typists and proud mothers, making war in an interactive dynamic with male warriors—and also victims of the universal dehumanization, rape and intimidation that men enact in war?

Another question arises: How can men be both heroic soldiers, fighting for homeland, family and the women back home, and also bullies committing insensitive and violent acts against women?

THE SYSTEMS APPROACH

The contradictions inherent in these questions bring us to search for a bigger perspective. At this point a systems approach is required that includes not just observable actions and interaction of different sectors of society or the myths that determine and give meaning to behavior patterns. We need a system that includes the overall psychological, cultural and social context that surrounds and often determines those actions, interactions and myths.

We live in a society that is founded upon myths and institutions that value and carry forth what has been defined as the "male principle," without benefit of the balancing effect of "feminine" values. Barbara Zanotti (1979) describes this society:

> Patriarchy is a system of dualisms: mind over body, thinking over feeling, heaven over earth, spirit over flesh–dualisms in which women are identified with the negative side. Patriarchy is a system of values developed through male experience: competition, hierarchy, aggression, bureaucracy, alienation from the earth, denial of emotion, generational shortsighted-ness, the objectification of the other.

Within the context of this kind of society, women are too often the unwitting–or witting–expressions of the narrow categorization of them as servers to men's goals, in anything. They are the nurses, mothers, typists and wives not just for warmaking, but for all endeavors. And they are prepared for these roles by a system–by the interactions they experience as infants, by their socialization, and by the roles made available to them. In other words, by psychology, economics, culture, social opportunity (or lack of it), and by force.

When war is declared, the need for community cohesion is magnified. The female personality that our society encourages presupposes women to the often invisible, "helping" roles that maintain the fabric of society in wartime. Plus, these roles often place women in positions where they are vulnerable, dependent, and easily victimized.

Our systems approach must recognize that men, too, are the unwitting–or witting–expressions of narrow categorizations of them. They are the soldiers, experts, leaders and protectors, locked into the feeling and behavior available to such roles. Men are prepared for them, again, by psychology, economics, culture, social opportunity (and lack of it), and by force.

Since the declaration of war always involves a series of splits into us-them, men-women, soldiers-civilians, godly-ungodly, the male finds it a mode consistent with his personality. When a young man enters the military, despite the grueling and authoritarian nature of basic training, he can find it a unique haven, psychologically speaking. While provided with food, shelter, entertainment and medical care, he can learn in an all-male setting what it is to be a man. The exclusion and degradation of women and female values is not accidental here. They are crucial parts of this system of "building men."

We may view warmaking and its escalation as a result of the patriarchal emphasis on competition, power-over and conquest. We may also view it as a result of the patriarchy's narrow categorization of human beings through rigid sex roles. In this kind of system, the loss of full human development for both women and men, may result in frustration, resentment, anger, grief, powerlessness, conflict, violence and lack of vision.

Ironically, in the context of this system, making war also provides the opportunity for women and men to become more whole human beings. Working in industry, business and the military, women have the chance to become physically and mentally more assertive, take risks and be independent. Likewise, men can experience an enlarging of their boundaries. They can touch each other, care for one another, and see their personal survival linked to communication, trust, and group cohesion. In light of these insights, we then wonder: Is war the best vehicle for offering psychic wholeness to human beings? Or, as Betty Reardon (1985) asks: Is peace even possible as long as patriarchal societies that split male from female dominate the globe?

Looking at this predicament from a pragmatic point of view, we could say that the very phenomena which the modern world needs to complement current values are those that women, as a class, know most about. In the Nuclear Age all human beings need, desperately, to remember our connection with one another–whether that be viewed as material connection through economic or ecological reality, or psychic connection through spiritual reality. We need to communicate our needs, our fears, our desires and our dreams. We need to subordinate the continuation of the game to the continuation of the relationship.

The absence of these "feminine" qualities and phenomena in the public forum has led to the excesses of our era. Were these same qualities to be reintroduced into our lives–not just in girls' games and at home, but at all levels of society–human survival would be more likely than it is today.

A rite of passage into the Nuclear Age for women, then, involves acknowledging, valuing and manifesting women's special concern for connection, relationship and communication on a societal level. To accomplish this, ironically, women must learn to selectively break the bonds of connection that they constantly seek. They must individuate enough, separate enough, develop ego boundaries enough, to bring their concern into the world.

Men encounter a different set of tasks. For them the problem is not that there is anything inherently wrong with the qualities and phenomena that have been cordoned off and called "male." Separateness, ego development and rationality are essential characteristics of human life and are crucial for the kind of thinking we must use if we are to survive, but in many societies they dominate and are not subject to the healthy balancing and complementary effect of those characteristics we call "female."

What we are called upon to do in the Nuclear Age is to undertake a rearrangement of psychological, cultural and social forces so that the male-dominated system by which we live does not arrive at its destined end point–a win-lose game leading to a lose-lose conclusion of nuclear weapons–but rather becomes more balanced and life-affirming. A rite of passage into this Age for men has to do with making this kind of transition. As for women, it involves acknowledging and validating what resources are already present: the will to individuate, the passion of the warrior, the desire to protect; but what is new is that this rite of passage cannot be complete until these qualities are manifested and honored in the context of connection and relationship.

As Shepherd Bliss (1985) has said, at this junction of history the value of men "shedding their armour" and "tending their wounds" is undeniable. With this tending comes an acceptance of the nurturing, reflective aspects of the male self, as well as direct, unprojected experience of the impulse behind violence against fellow living beings. Male involvement in child rearing and care also breaks the cycle of patriarchal development, offering the male adult the opportunity to explore, nurturance and connection. Plus, it gives both boy and girl children the chance to relate to and identify with the male, and to grow into more whole human beings.

At this point we are well aware that "male" cultural configurations stand challenged by the nuclear reality. While the ultimate bomb may have been the technological device that destroyed Hiroshima, the ultimate "sex bomb" was Rita Hayworth, a decal-picture of her body glued to that bomb as it was dropped from the belly of the Enola Gay, a plane named for the commander's mother. In these times it becomes clear that militarism and sexism emanate from the same system of thought and that this system must change. The old myth of the male warrior-hero no longer works. There is no more triumph in winning. There is no more separating oneself out, and no more putting down women in the process. As Mark Getzon (1983) has written: "The frontiersman now becomes the healer, the soldier becomes the mediator; the breadwinner becomes the companion; the expert becomes the nurturer."

As we embark upon these rites of passage, women and men join together to reduce the world's nuclear arsenal; to ask questions about our myth of war and peace, women and men: and to accomplish change–not just in policy, but on all levels of our human being. In these times both sexes need protection, and the talents of both sexes are needed to protect our endangered planet. Working together we stand at the fragile edge of a vision–a world made up of more whole women and men no longer engaged in the battle of the sexes.

*OPPOSITES ATTRACT**

Girl attracts boy. Boy pursues. Girl resists. Boy persists. Probably the most widespread conflict in human history, and for many people no doubt the most fun. Flirting and romance, subject of vast volumes of literature down through the ages, seems to be driven by two basic urges–the feminine urge to attract and tempt, and the masculine urge to conquer and dominate.

These urges that can excite us in love, often divide us in society. They spice up the inner workings of our social groups, but indiscriminate spice often ruins the entire meal. Flirting and romance in inappropriate places at inappropriate times with inappropriate

---

* Adapted from existing Earthview Press publications and from reference material (Gilligan) cited in Chapter 10.

people can generate friction and conflicts in our schools, clubs, companies . . . in any social systems where males and females interact.

Besides discretion, the secret to peace between the genders is to maintain respect for and knowledge of the opposite sex. Here are some of the things modern psychologists are learning about masculine and feminine aspects.

Children's games. Boys tend to play competitive games outdoors in large groups. The games are often long-lasting and involve a lot of skill. Disputes break out fairly often, but boys seem to enjoy resolving conflicts as much as playing the game. Boys are preoccupied by game rules, referring to them frequently to work out disputes. While playing, boys learn competitiveness, independence, and organizational skills that will be helpful later in life in coordinating the activities of large, diverse groups. Meanwhile, girls like to play indoors, usually in small, intimate groups. The games are less competitive, more cooperative, and when disputes break out the girls usually end the game rather than threaten the relationships. Girls are more flexible than boys; they are more likely to bend the rules and adopt any changes that will result in greater fairness and less pain all around. Girls learn to cooperate smoothly while nurturing and preserving interpersonal relationships. They become open-minded.

Law and morality. Women generally have a more difficult time than men making moral decisions because they consider many variables. They analyze a situation, looking for the "right"option–the one that will cause the least conflict and pain. Men seem to prefer making hastier, more rational decisions. They eliminate many variables by creating legal and moral boundaries and rules. To make the "right" decision they simply consult the rulebooks. They want quick, neat justice . . . even if it sometimes causes pain to individuals and puts a strain on relationships. Women want to nurture healthy relationships, even if it requires more time, more creativity, and a bending of rules to come up with the "right" solution.

Communication. Women tend to express their feelings openly. Men generally do not. Girls while away hour after teenage hour exchanging their feelings and analyzing relationships over the phone or in hushed, excited conversations. Boys talk about cars, girls, sports, studies . . . virtually anything but their feelings. Boys and girls each think that the other gender's subjects of discussion are trivial.

Interpersonal fears. If men and women were to make separate lists of the social conditions they fear most, women might have a sense of separation and isolation near the top of their list, along with being held in suspicion or being rejected by others for being too successful and competitive. Men might have among their greatest fears feeling entrapped or betrayed, humiliated by deceit, and smothered in a clingy relationship. Coming together intimidates men, while moving apart intimidates women . . . a situation reminiscent of the combined forces of the sun's gravity and our planet's centrifugal force—one trying to pull our solar system together while the other tries to pull it apart. If either force were to prevail, the system would be destroyed, but when working together they keep our sun and Earth in comfortable harmony.

A peaceful world will require the efforts and skills of both genders working together in comfortable harmony, in mutual respect and understanding.

REFERENCES

Bliss, S. (1985). "Men, wounding and war." Paper presented at Self, Society and Nuclear Conflict conference. University of California, San Francisco/Langley Porter Psychiatric Institute, October 19-20, 1985, in San Francisco, Calif.

Brownmiller, S. (1976). *Against our will: men, women and rape.* New York: Bantam Books.

Campbell. J. (1980). *Myths to live by.* New York: Bantam Books.

Chodorow, N. (1978). *The reproduction of mothering: psychoanalysis and the sociology of gender.* Berkeley. Calif.: University of California Press.

Dinnerstein, D. (1976). *The mermaid and the minotaur.* New York: Harper Calaphon Books.

Gerzon, M. (1983). *A choice of heroes.* New York: Houghton Mifflin.

Glendinning, C. (1987). *Waking up in the nuclear age.* New York: William Morrow and Company.

Gilligan, C. (1982). *In a different voice: psychological theory and women's development.* Cambridge. Mass.: Harvard University Press.

Harman, W. (1984). "Peace on earth: The impossible dream become possible." *Journal of human psychology* 24 (3) pp. 77-92.

Kohlberg, L. (1969). "Stage and sequence: The cognitive-development approach to socialization." In D.A. Goslin (Ed.), Handbook of socialization theory and research. Chicago: Rand McNally.

Lorenz, K. (1966). *On aggression.* New York: Bantam Books.

Reardon, B. (1981). *Sexism and the war system.* New York: Teachers College press.

Stiehm, J. (1982). "The protected, the protector, the defender." Women's studies international forum 5, pp. 367-76.

Zanotti, B. (1979). "Militarism and violence: A feminist perspective." Paper presented at Riverside Church Disarmament Conference, New York.

Zur, O. (1985). "Men, women and war." Paper presented at the Western Psychological Association annual conference, April, San Jose, Calif.

Zur O. (1989). War Myths. J. Humanistic Psychology 29/3, 247-327.

Zur O., & Morrison, A. (1989).Gender and War: Re Examining Attitudes, *American Journal of Orthopsychiatry,* V. 59(4): 523-533.

Metanoia:
A Great Change of Heart

Gail Kadison Golden

SUMMARY. The author draws on her experience working with individual men who are violent to their partners to think about the problem of international violence. A parallel is drawn between a man's feeling of "entitlement" to forcefully keep his partner "in line" and feelings of national entitlement to engage in violence to force one group's agenda on another. The differences between morals and taboos are discussed underscoring the community value of that which becomes socially and ethically "unthinkable."

For quite a number of years now, I have worked at a family counseling center which has, as part of its mission, to serve clients of the family court. Because of this affiliation, my colleagues and I have had to develop expertise in those issues which clients began to present with great frequency. Domestic violence became, perhaps, the problem most regularly touching the lives of the clients referred to our agency. Thus, beginning back in the '70s we began a long process of immersion in this most difficult problem in order to learn how to be most helpful to our women clients who were being battered, and then to the men who were doing the battering. The agency became part of a grass roots network addressing the problem, and today, though a rather small agency, offers service, expertise, and training which is a model for the entire state of New York.

In looking at the problem of violence over the years we asked

Gail Kadison Golden is a practicing psychotherapist and Clinical Director of the Volunteer Counseling Service of Rockland County, NY. She is the author of a number of professional articles and a published poet. Correspondence may be addressed to 18 Zabella Drive, New City, NY 10956.

27

many questions. What caused it; why did men beat the women they had promised to cherish; how could we protect her; how could we get him to stop? In time, because this is a social work agency, we were also asking larger questions. In what social context can domestic abuse exist in such large numbers that it almost constitutes a norm?

The analysis we began to work with was that developed by the New York State Coalition against domestic violence. This analysis was supported and enriched by the research and hands on work of women and men across the country who took up the challenge of this most disturbing problem. Over time a number of points became clear. Men do not commit acts of violence against their partners because of reasons previously upheld. Men do not abuse because of poor relationships with their mother, problems with their fathers, early deprivation or trouble at the job. It is not an intrapsychic problem. Nor are we looking at sadomasochistic pairings, in which one person theoretically needs and wants to be hit and thus finds a partner willing to do so. Men do not abuse because they are in pathological relationships. They also do not use violence because of the behaviors of their partners. The trigger is random, elusive, and changes from day to day, house to house. That is to say, men do not hit because the behavior of their partners is so noxious as to leave no choice. Men do not hit because of a problem in the marital system. Nor do they hit because they drink, or because of social class, ethnicity, educational background, religious affiliation, or financial circumstances.

Men hit because we all live in a sexist and patriarchal culture which not only allows and tolerates such behavior, but which historically has encouraged it. A man's home has been his castle, his wife and children have been his property and his duty has been to keep all of them "in line." The range of institutions designed to maintain social norms, the police, the judges, the clergy, the doctors, the mental health workers, and the social workers were for many years part of a large social collaboration to uphold the family and to keep the woman in her place. Her place was taking care of her home, her children and her mate, trying to please, and deferring to the head of the house. In this context violence was justified by the misdeed, poor judgment, or problematic behavior of the women (she asked for it).

Men hit because the culture has rested on an assumption of justifiable and permissible violence committed by the dominant group, males, against the subordinate group, females. In short, men batter because they think they can. They tend to work on stopping this behavior when it becomes clear to them that abuse of their partners is neither justified nor permitted by the community. This is a significant paradigm shift for men who have grown up in a patriarchal culture, inheriting assumptions of entitlement and rights of dominance. The shift requires strong confronting reeducation which clearly places responsibility for the violence on those who commit the violent acts. The shift also requires strong community consensus. Violent behavior towards partners is no longer legal behavior in many communities. It is not tolerated by the police, nor the judges. Abusers can and will be arrested.

In other words, domestic violence has the most possibility of stopping when it progresses away from being a social norm and moves towards becoming a social taboo, that which is unthinkable. Men who are violent towards their partners need to come to see that there are no circumstances which require a violent response. In addition, the community must support a stance that it does not condone violent acts. Despite all of the interventions and treatment strategies designed to reduce violent behavior, the single most effective means of stopping abuse is to arrest the perpetrators. In other words, the community needs to provide a stern superego. It appears that those superego controls are eroded or are never completely formed in individuals who are born and raised in a patriarchal culture. How does this analysis impact on violence between nations?

As long as we hold to a set of facile justifications for war, we will have no way to stop it. The mind set is one which understands many reasons for a "just" war. And once that war is understood as just it also becomes not only okay but even heroic, a cause for celebration.

In 1992 we require a paradigm shift. We need the mind to understand that war is always tragic, representing a total failure of human possibility. When we try to stop individual men from being violent to their mates, we begin by telling them that it is never all right to commit violent acts towards a partner. In the same way we need to begin to know that it is never all right to go to war.

It is not glorious. It is always an atrocity. Also it is not always as justifiable as we like to think. Wars fought for territory, natural resources, trade routes, oil, religious fundamentalism need to become unthinkable. The provocation of the other (she made me do it) never relieves us of the obligation and responsibility to find another way to resolve conflict. Violence is too easy. Once we say, comfortably, that it is all right in certain circumstances, the list of circumstances will grow exponentially. If we understand that it is never all right, we will begin to have the mind to struggle towards other means of resolving conflict. The Most Venerable Nichidatsu Fujii writes:

> Skill and machines are required to take the lives of others; yet, in order not to take the lives of others, no skills or machines are necessary. It is enough to accept and maintain the precept of non-killing. When this is accepted deeply, the mind to hate nuclear weapons, to reject war, will appear. Through this, the future of humankind shall be illuminated by survival and prosperity without fears. (Postcard, 1985)

It is tempting to be simplistic about this. But in our century the reality of Hitler and Pearl Harbor are haunting. These memories present serious problems for those adhering to antimilitary principles. The necessity to respond in literal self defense or the need to halt the progress of a truly malevolent leader persist as severe tests of the intention to wage peace rather than war. These are extremes.

In the individual realm we "allow" for violence against another when one's own life is being threatened. Because our culture demands extensive justification of such defensive actions they do not occur routinely.

We need to begin to make it extremely difficult, if not impossible to justify violence on an international scale. The potential for nuclear destruction and for the ravaging of the earth's ecosystem clarify the unsupportable nature of modern warfare, even in situations which we are convinced we can "win."

In her book *Purity and Danger* (1966) anthropologist Mary Douglas differentiates between community morals and community taboos. Morals refer to the agreed upon behavioral ideals of the group. Behaviors which are taboo are those which are seen to be dangerous to the social group, defiling the group by contact with an abomination.

Thus, for example, our social morals direct people towards marital fidelity, though it is understood that many people do not achieve this ideal. Sexual activity between an adult and a child, however, is a taboo, and perpetrators are regarded as criminals.

Douglas suggests that when moral indignation is not reinforced by political sanctions, then concepts of taboo can be marshalled to provide a deterrent. When a sense of community outrage is equipped with practical sanctions in the social order, the necessity to treat the behavior as taboo is not likely to arise. When outrages go unpunished, the concept of that which is forbidden tends to be called upon to supplement the lack of other sanctions.

With the whole planet in danger from our increasingly sophisticated weapons, we need the mind to see war as the abomination that it is, the abomination which defiles the victors and victims alike, that act which has the potential for making the whole earth impure.

When our sense of ethical and moral behavior has eroded severely, powerful external sanctions need to be marshalled. Thus, when there was the recognition that the patriarchal value system justified an epidemic of domestic violence, the need for strong community disapproval and sanction became clearer. As we increasingly recognize that the same value system justifies armed conflict and ecological destruction we need to struggle in a similar direction.

Scientist Thomas Kuhn suggests that a shift in communal vision, or a paradigm shift, occurs when an anomaly awakens us to new questions (1970). Theologian Matthew Fox states: "The war on nature and on Mother Earth that proceeds unabatedly and without interference by organized religion provides a startling anomaly indeed" (1988). Another startling anomaly is provided by a recent U.S. Senate Judiciary Committee Report which states: The United States is the "most violent and self-destructive nation on earth." U.S. Citizens are "killing, raping and robbing one another at a furious rate, surpassing every other country that keeps records" (Fellowship Magazine, Dec. 1991, p. 26).

Kuhn and Fujii maintain that it is the growing awareness that something is terribly amiss in one's world view which produces breakthrough. I see it as not only a reorientation of vision but a paradigm shift that will involve a metanoia, a great change of heart. Let us hope this volume can contribute to that growing awareness.

REFERENCES

Douglas, M. (1966). *Purity and danger.* London: Henley Routledge & Kegan Paul.
Fox, M. (1988). *The coming of the cosmic Christ.* NY: Harper & Row.
Kuhn, T. (1970). *The structure of scientific revolutions.* Chicago: The University of Chicago Press.
U.S. Senate Judiciary Committee Report in *Fellowship Magazine,* Dec. 1991, Nyack, NY.

We Have Failed

Norman F. Shub

SUMMARY. This article explores the changing nature of the psychotherapeutic world in relationship to the values crisis evident in our lack of reaction to the Gulf War. It attempts to examine the underlying valuelessness of the new post-modern psychotherapeutic systems with special attention to the impact of that changing value structure on humanistic psychotherapy, the mental health community and the significance of this shifting as it relates to the Gulf War. The author examines these philosophic systems that underlie various post-modern approaches and their challenge to universal humanism and humanistic values. Finally the reader is encouraged to reassess the underlying value base of their therapeutic, methodological, and philosophical systems.

INTRODUCTION

As I watched the upsurge of Nationalism and so-called Patriotism in the wake of the Gulf War, I began to realize to what degree we have failed. The outbreak of excitement, enthusiasm for pain, suffering and death reminded me of a short story. In this story, a

---

Norman F. Shub, BCD, author, teacher, psychotherapist, is Director of the nationally known Center for the Treatment of Character, located in Columbus, OH. Norman has had extensive therapeutic experience and has led workshops throughout the United States, Canada, the Middle East, Europe, South America, etc. His books, *The Process of Character Work* series will be published beginning in 1993. He is also on the editorial board of various journals including, *Voices, the Journal of the American Academy of Psychotherapists*. Norman is currently serving as clinical director of the post-graduate faculty of the Gestalt Associates, a private practice group dedicated to the highest quality depth therapy.

33

young boy is caught lying on his living room rug watching piranhas tear to shreds some goldfish he had purchased at a local pet store. Upon being asked why he did this horrible thing, the young boy replied, "Well, I heard about piranhas and I just had to see what it would be like to watch them."

I was terribly saddened and disappointed to watch my neighbors and friends put our flag out in front of their homes symbolizing their support for an exhibition of violence which in their words, they "clearly did not understand." Unlike Vice-President Quayle, whose concern with valuelessness is limited to "special groups," my concern is for our country, our populace as a whole. It was the underlying valuelessness of his behavior that horrified this latency aged boy's parents when he purchased the bag of goldfish to watch them die. It is my contention that this valuelessness is a brushfire burning out of control in the universal psyche of our country.

As Frank Pittman has noted in *The Family Therapy Networker*, one of the greatest present dangers to our purported humanistic value base is the contextualist, philosophical and theoretical movement. As Pittman has noted in an ascerbic look at contextualist therapy,

> All views of reality become equally real—or unreal—as the case may be. Reality has become a matter of opinion. I'm reminded of the postmodern hippie in the movie *Atlantic City* who refused to wear a seat belt on an airplane because she didn't believe in gravity. I understand those who seek sureness in rigid fundamentalism.
>
> Postmodernism entered family therapy in the form of constructivism, espousing that reality is in the eye of the beholder, and that it doesn't matter what people do, only what story they tell to change what they do! They can just use intellectual masturbation, until we notice that the world that constructivism is defining away is a cruel, unsafe, unfair place that hurts real people. Constructivists can seem like Republicans: defining away poverty, AIDS, homelessness, inequality. (1992, pg. 58)

This upsurge in enthusiasm for the Gulf War is a perfect example of our country's intoxication with the same post-modern/contextualist thinking. There are the good guys and the bad guys. There is right and wrong. There is no truth and thus no untruth. We refocus the lens and the problem is gone.

WHERE HAVE ALL THE VALUES GONE, LONG TIME PASSING

As we begin to think about this concern over values, we wonder where are the impassioned leaders of the humanistic movements of the 60s and 70s who espoused a completely different set of values. *These values* which fly in the face of much that has happened in the last several years—why aren't they being espoused? The truth is that we have failed. We have failed to help people to continue to be aware. We have failed to help people to understand the nature of humanism, and the values of humane relationships. We have failed to help people to understand the process of conflict and conflict resolution in a humane way. We currently are failing to stand and uphold the torch for the values that we all, at one point, were willing to protest about. Conceptualist couples and family therapy is the superficial symptom of some of the deeper value erosion brought on by a shift in commitment to the importance of a meaningful value base.

HOW HAVE WE FAILED?

As the anti-humanistic poison has seeped through the doors and windows of Academia, foundation principles have been challenged, overlooked, discarded in the social sciences, mental health profession, and in our political leadership. In his groundbreaking essay in the *Public Interest*, Joel Schwartz (1990, pg. 30) discussing Luc Ferry and Alain Renaut, notes:

> Ferry and Renaut's concept of post-modern antihumanism is important because it focuses squarely on the central defect of the schools of thought that they examine. The most crucial failing of these schools is not their stylistic difficulty or their

fondness for jargon, but rather their vision of humanity—a vision that explicitly rejects the very possibility of truth, morality, and rationality.

Our underlying philosophical base has shifted away from fundamental humanism. Our professionals, our leadership have lost touch with and sight of the core values which brought us together, the values which moved us to be concerned with creating a more caring world. When those sentiments are expressed, they are seen as supercilious, trivialized, and are lost in the narcissism of the 80s, the directionlessness of the 90s. Our post-modern marital and family therapists are utilizing a theoretical system that has been adapted from these specific philosophical systems and may be unaware of the underlying challenge to fundamental core values that these systems represent. Is our profession aware of the growing need for a reevaluation of our fundamental values and a deeper understanding of how that value base is expressed through theory, methodology, in small and large systems? As we have noted above, many of the past and present leadership of the mental health community have identified with the political left, which after all, has considered itself the "party of humanity." As Schwartz (1990, pg. 30) has gone on to note:

> thus it (the deconstructionist) has criticized society for dehumanizing the individuals who compose it, and specifically for preventing the poor and underprivileged from achieving the mental and moral excellence that is potentially theirs. In that spirit, the left has striven for the liberation of mankind, to be achieved through the creation of a truly universal society in which the human dignity of all would be recognized.

The post-modern/contextualist thinking that currently appeals to Academia considers the ideals of truth, human excellence, universality a joke. How can this vision of mankind, this dark view be so popular and so accepted by individuals who once stood for opposite values?

As we explore more precisely some of the key concerns that must be addressed in this examination of our current beliefs, I would also like to raise the specter of the *influence* these theoretical/philosophical systems have on issues critical to our profession, issues such as managed care, lack of insurance, and the fundamental questioning of the value of depth relationship-oriented therapy. It is my belief that these philosophical constructs and their concommitant theoretical systems support, if not engender the notion of extremely limited mental health services, as well as question the validity of depth psychotherapy as a process. As Pittman (1992, pg. 58) says, we can't story tell away AIDS, poverty or post-traumatic stress.

As we think about the families of the Gulf War soldiers, for example, and the post-traumatic reactions they may have incurred, it is important to realize that these theoretical approaches will prohibit our military from receiving the breadth, length and depth of treatment that they need to recover from a war which many did not understand in the first place.

Let us examine more closely some of the values that are being rejected so that we might consider a recommitment to humanism.

IS TRUTH VALUED?

One of the leading lights of this post-modern movement is Jacque Derrida (1976) who has had a tremendous influence on western thinking. Derrida, one of the main proponents of deconstructionism, believes that man cannot meaningfully discuss the objective world. Furthermore, he believes that we don't have the capacity to say something about our own feelings. According to Derrida (1976) we cannot truly describe the world of ourselves and ourselves in the world. Derrida (1976) insists that our inability to deal with truth, common human experiences, arrive at any sort of universal meaning that might ground human reason or moral action is *no calamity.* Instead, it is a liberation from the logocentric repression under which he thinks we have previously suffered. Others may have thought that the truth will make you free, Derrida contends that only the absence or the impossibility of truth can liberate.

The deconstructionistic posits that there are no universal truths and thus, our basic, human experiences become momentary exchanging contexts. Situational ethics/symbolism as human experience supplants the fundamental value base that we have struggled to work from. In the humanistic/psychotherapeutic revolution of the 60s, we shared common beliefs, ideals and what we consider truths about life in our world. If truths are deemed non-existent by the irrationalist, then our common bond is broken as *our clear goals become diffused or non-existent.*

As we examine *our* perceptions of the Gulf War and the constantly shifting realities of who is *good* and who is *bad,* we see evidence of irrationalist/deconstructionist thinking and its imprint on our post-modern world. What is psychotherapy without universal truths, and what are psychotherapists without the ability to struggle with people regarding these universal truths?

THE NEGATION OF HUMAN COMMUNICATION

There is certainly nothing wrong with Derrida's arguing that human reason is severely limited; it is obvious that many great philosophers have taken that position. There is, however, something deeply wrong with his complacent refusal to find anything problematic in the radical limitations on human communication that follow from his analysis. To argue as Derrida does that language defeats human intentions, yet to be untroubled by that conclusion, is to contradict oneself as well as to trivialize the human condition. Schwartz (1990, pp. 33-34)

As psychotherapists of family and marital therapy, we are constantly encouraging people to learn to communicate more effectively. Thus, we value the efficacy of human communication. Derrida proffers the notion that language does not enable us to comprehend a reality beyond itself. Language, as understood by Derrida, is a process that is continually changing over time as the attempt to make sense of words is put off or deferred. Language is seen as self contradictory and human communication is a non-transcendent event. If communication is impossible, as Derrida implies, we should all follow the dictum of Woody Allen who makes a similar point when he observes that people who talk about the impossibility of communicating to "just shut up." As Schwartz (1990, pg. 35) goes on to note:

Derrida may believe that the inability to communicate, to express our intentions comprehensively, indicates that we have booked past the *Love Boat*; it is far more likely, however, that the vessel is the *Titanic*.

If we allow this irrationalism to seep into the methodology of psychotherapy then our attempts at valuing human communication are for naught. Teaching couples to communicate, teaching groups to communicate, teaching people to communicate thus becomes an exercise in futility. If we subscribe to Derrida's philosophy, then post-modern psychotherapy would become irrationally contextualist and pushed to the extreme, imply that an individual could only understand a symbol in that moment and therefore human communication as we now know it, is defunct.

Thus, as Derrida, and others have noted, the efficacy of basic communication is non-existent. What one person says to another is both transitory and meaningless over time.

Derrida's chief concern is with language, which he presents as an inherently fluid and unstable medium. Rather than controlling language, we are largely controlled by it. 'The subject . . . always say[s] . . . more, less, or something other than what he *would mean* [Derrida's italics].' In part this is because we cannot use language to describe an external reality that transcend language. Schwartz (1990, pg. 34)

How many of us would practice therapy utilizing this frame?

HOPE?

If there is no universal truth, no universal values, and the efficacy of human communication is challenged, we as psychotherapists can offer no hope for the post-modern world. The vision of this world put forth by Derrida is forbidding. Schwartz (1990, pg. 30) suggests that "there is something facetious in Derrida's wholesale rejection of universalism, and in fact we ask him for the most arbitrary, willful individualism." In this post-modern dark world, the individual is crushed by the yoke of uncertainty of language. The obscuring of language empowers him to tyrannize it, interpreting freely to make of it what he will. The meeting of these two extremes is no coincidence. Mastery, like slavery, denies to men the capacity to seek and be understood by one another and on that basis, to frame and abide by universal moral laws . . . thus there is no hope.

If we subscribe to this philosophical system and the concommitant methodology for change that it has engendered, we find that relationship-oriented therapy does not offer the hope of being the ground for being different. Since human communication is not valued, is not universal, the *relationship* between the therapist and the patient is not particularly helpful nor unique. As a profession we have always stood for the efficacy of human relationship. How can we stand by and let such notions seep into the context of our methodology?

Once again, if human communication is not universal, and the meaning of a statement cannot transcend the moment, then the fabric of *marital therapy* must be reexamined and changed. This frighteningly bleak notion about human relationship leads to contempt for the human spirit and the efficacy of human life. If we adopt this stark view, then the work with couples that we have struggled to understand and learn about is in question. Trust is a fundamental value, as well as a building block of the entire psychotherapeutic world. If we no longer value trust as a human experience, then the reactions to the Gulf War and its existence make more sense. In this post-modern age where trust might be no longer valued, the only solution to serious conflict is combat, annihilation, or some form of not understanding the other. Dispute resolution, arbitration, negotiation, and other human processes which rely on trust lose their meaning.

WHERE ARE WE?

Can we overlook the fact that we have not stood up and cried out for reevaluation and reexamination of our values as humanism has seeped away, eroded by post-modern poison? How can we allow issues such as poverty, racism, sexism, and other incredibly important and vital concerns of our society be trivialized with the notion that if you change your view, you change your problem? Who believes this?

The values that we have espoused and examined are values which we believe must underlie the psychotherapeutic movement in the United States. It is this author's belief that the erosion of these values, acceptance of alternate philosophical/methodological/theoretical and clinical systems from which they are engendered have eroded our value base to the point where atrocities, such as the Gulf War can take place without our profession batting an eye. As I sit in my study and write this article, I realize that for most of us the Gulf War is forgotten, a part of history, it is not in our awareness. This is a tragedy, for if we once again hold up a live torch for humanistic values, the lesson of the Gulf War which is that it flew in the face of all the values which the human potential psychotherapy movement stands for, would not be forgotten.

This article is appearing in this collection in which numerous articles are founded on principles such as trust, universal truths, hope, caring for one another. Can we go on and allow the important beliefs to erode as we move into the contextualist/post-modern/deconstructionist age? I hope not.

REFERENCES

Derrida, J. (1976) *Of Grammatolog.* (G.C. Spivak, trans.) Baltimore: Johns Hopkins University Press (Originally published, 1972.)

Pittman, F. (1992) It's not my fault. *The Family Therapy Networker,* Jan/Feb, *16* (1), 58.

Schwartz, J. (1990) Antihumanism in the humanities. *The Public Interest, 10,* 29-44.

There Is But One Love We Share

Margaret Kirschner

SUMMARY. The spiritual void of our culture, the dependency that maintains the isolation, and gives rise to the violence that permeates from individual to personal relationships to national policy, is examined. As an antidote, the article explores development of inner lives of awareness and connectedness with all that exists that begins with each person, leads to the qualities that are the groundwork for peaceful relationships. Special emphasis is given to the moral responsibility of clinicians who hope to be serving others.

The title's simple wisdom floated in to me one spring day, inscribed on the wedding invitation of dear friends. Like a Native American who treasures a feather (the symbolic gift of wisdom), I hold this thought close to my heart.

My wish for my friends was that they would always have a full experience of the One Love that animates all the creatures of the earth, the earth itself, and the love that flows from that unity. Even as I wished, I was also aware of the environment in which they would be living in which the unity is often ignored or disregarded. During my years as a psychotherapist, over and over I have heard the presenting complaints of clients who express how lonely they feel, how unsupported, how misunderstood they are. I observe their isolation, whether from anger or passivity, and feel the pain of its effects on their lives.

From birth we all yearn to belong. Yet some feel so apart they seriously wonder if they haven't come from another planet. Others

---

Margaret Kirschner, MEd, Licensed Professional Counselor and Board Certified Psychotherapist with Diplomate standing, is recently retired from her professional career in private practice and industry consultation, and her work at Emanuel Pain Center. Her new focus will be on writing and theater arts.

wander aimlessly, stating "I don't know who I am, or what I'm supposed to be doing. I don't even know what I want." They express only their emptiness. "I feel like there is a big black hole inside me." The lonely meaninglessness has become a national characteristic, or in the words of Frieda Fordham (1953) "the general neuroses of our time." But, for all of us, it is as Goethe expressed, "Being a (person) is a search for the home where we dwell." If not stronger than the sexual drive, surely more enduring is the need to belong. Finding our home is the task that leads us on, expands our lives, readies us for death. It is our human condition.

For those of us living in twentieth century America, the search for belonging is often desperate. How often people look to a relationship to ease their loneliness. Harmonious or not, they cling as if for their lives, as we hear reflected in popular songs that wail out how "I need you–I can't live without you," etc. Yet frequently the relationships break up and people go on from one to another to another, or for some, to several at a time. Our songs just as often bemoan the "how could you leave me" syndrome. Too often sex is sought as a palliative for loneliness. Like a drug, one encounter cries for another in search of satiation. Relief becomes more illusive with each sexual exploitation. At some point, the "right one" is found, the one who will cure their loneliness, and they marry. Based on that false assumption (spelled out by Dr. Don Jackson [1968]), the ensuing marriage is a tragic disappointment, a fairy tale with an unhappy ending, consistent with our national statistics that tell us one out of every two marriages ends in divorce (Census Bureau, 1991). During those marriages, the disappointment, frustration, resentment that follow contribute to the shocking data that show the violence visited upon the children. Estimates range from three to four out of five of our daughters are physically and sexually abused. Coming to light more recently, statistics regarding our sons are less clear, but the evidence points to a high rate of abuse that they endure. When divorce enters, it spells poverty for the higher percentage of the single parents (usually the mothers) and their children. This is an abuse of neglect set up by our economic interests, governmental indifference, and the apathy of an isolated citizenry. Rather than being supported, a single mother is handicapped by jobs that pay her 69 cents for every dollar a man earns, and often deprives her of healthcare, forcing her and her children into the high percentage of the 35 million Americans who go without medical coverage (Census Bureau, 1991). The cost of daycare begins at $300.00 a month. Who in our population is left to care for the elderly, either with time or money?

Among the marriages that last, many are unhappy. The partners, too dependent to separate (the stable-unhappy marriages, the "worst of the lot" [Jackson, 1963]), endure one another, isolated in their own worlds of suffering. The hostilities may be masked by a "happy" front. The angers are not admitted, the fighting is hidden behind sweet smiles, "helpful" postures, and false optimism. The children suffer the sad effects of the joyless marriage and are as lonely as their parents. They learn the same dependent behaviors that interlock their parents into a veritable prison, to carry on in their relationships throughout life.

Finding their marriages sadly awry, many turn to religion for the answer. Sociologist Andrew Greeley (1991) reports that, contrary to popular opinion, " . . . more than 95 out of every 100 people believe in God, three out of every four believe in the divinity of Jesus Christ, three out of five believe in hell, two out of five go to church once a week, nine out of ten pray every week, one out of two prays every day." What then is the frightening discrepancy between the statistics of American family, societal, national life and the high numbers of believers and church goers?

There is an unmet expectation, like the false assumptions of marriage, that going to church will magically solve our problems. In our religions, rather than on a mere mortal, we put our hopes on a Being with supernatural powers, to fix things for us–or perhaps more accurately, to be our fix. As Father Leo Booth (1991) explains, "The 'great lie' of addiction and co-dependency is that something external, beyond us, will make life better, something beyond us will make us feel good, acceptable, lovable and worthwhile. The more we believe in a 'fixer,' the more dependent we grow on that external source. . . . Religious addicts feel that God sees them as dirty and sinful, so they make others feel dirty and sinful. Religious addicts feel like victims of God's whims, so they victimize and abuse others. . . . Religious addiction, like alcoholism, springs from a reservoir of low self-esteem, inadequacy, shame, guilt and the desire to escape, fix or numb these feelings." While we wait for God to fix it, the divorce rates climb, drug and alcohol abuse runs rampant, violent crimes increase, hate crimes rise, and 87% of our nation supported the Gulf War! The alienation of the individual spreads outward to all relationships, families, religions, community and governmental institutions. The American public has lost faith in its leaders–after all, they are cut from the same cloth as the rest of us. The idea of turning to our government for support is laughable to most of us. Our values have become jaded, we believe might makes right, our imagined needs justified killing hundreds of thousands of Iraqi civilians. Recall the increasing references to morality and nobility under God's patronage that President Bush made as he pulled us closer into war. Such sanctimonious jargon puts a double bind upon the people who, sincerely wishing to do the right thing, are asked to participate in the carnage in God's name. It would seem that the Gulf War fulfilled Antigone's predictions, "You would make of it a cemetery and call it peace."

Still we search. We are a nation of people yearning for belonging. In its absence, *we suffer a profound spiritual void.* We have religion/s, but do we have spiritual lives? We believe in God, but do we experience God? Where and how are we taught to experience the ineffable? How many of us develop a deep inner life? How many of us enjoy our internal beauty and strength?

Marriages, families, religious and governmental institutions are not offering us the belonging we ache for because *we* are still functioning with the personalities appropriate for a hierarchal society regardless of our verbal commitment to the contrary. We behave as dependent children, passively following or angrily rebelling, either way blindly and impotently. Sadly, I observe many of those who "freed" themselves from an authoritarian marriage or belief system, clinging just as dependently to a new spouse or a new doctrine. We continue to expect others to give us a sense of belonging. We expect someone or something to relieve our loneliness while we remain unaware of where or how to experience the deep sense of communion with ultimate reality that is available to us. A dependent attitude permits others to do our thinking. We live on the surface of our lives. Because this is contradictory to our natures, we avoid the contradiction by keeping desperately busy, climbing social or economic ladders, being consumers, playing harder. If all else fails, we turn to drink and drugs to dull our minds, or to religion, or to food, or to relationships–it doesn't matter what we do so long as we can prevent ourselves from becoming aware. We develop an addictive lifestyle to avoid the deeper truths that await our discovery. For an indepth study of the way dependence leads to a pattern of co-dependence, I refer the reader to Anne Wilson Schaef's *Co-Dependence* (1986). To follow the development of an addictive lifestyle as it permeates every facet of our society until the institutions themselves promote co-dependence (or is it the other way around?), one can read her illuminating *When Society Becomes an Addict* (1987).

The question, then, is how do we find a sense of belonging in our culture? Further, how do we as therapists empower our clients to do this?

Each of us must begin to develop a deep interior life. To do so it is essential to concentrate our attention inward. We are each a manifestation of the One Love. There is but One Reality to which we belong. This is a tenet of all major world religions. It is the finding of the quantum physicists. Einstein discovered space/time to be one continuum. David Bohm (1975, p. 93) expanded the continuum: "Ultimately, the entire universe (with all its "particles," including those constituting human beings, their laboratories, observing instruments, etc.) has to be understood as a single undivided whole, in which analysis into separately and independently existent parts has no fundamental status." Each of us is a Microcosm of the Whole. We become aware of what a minute bit of the whole we are while paradoxically we know the whole does not exist without us. Paradoxes are seen on a continuum. It is simultaneously humbling and exalting to experience the merging of this polarity, as did Blake (1964, p. 40) when he saw "a universe in a grain of sand." Despite the uniqueness of each one of us, we are all interconnected, animated by the same universal energy that animates everything else, fish and fowl, animals and insects, water and earth. It is impossible to be "independent" though we can experience isolation when we are unaware of our belonging. We are, therefore, our own best workshop to begin the journey of discovering our belonging, our home.

Getting to know the Ultimate Reality by looking within may seem overwhelming, baffling as to how to begin. Fortunately, the process is simple and available to all of us. It merely requires consistent attention. Not always easy, but simple. Observe, for example, a small child who becomes transfixed by a ladybug. Nothing interrupts his/her attention. S/he comes away from that watchfulness with a thousand and one questions, "Why does it have more legs than we do?" "Where are its ears?" "Who painted the spots on it?" "Where does it live?" "Can it talk?" Chances are, the child may try to walk like the ladybug, or flap his/her arms like wings. And so the child ponders the mystery of life, learning from that moment in time when s/he merged with a ladybug.

An inspiring description of a child's mystical experience has been given to us by Mary Austin (1932, p. 371) in her autobiography:

> It must be understood that to me God *is* the experienceable quality in the universe . . .
>
> I must have been between five and six when this experience happened to me. It was a summer morning and the child that I was had walked down through the orchard alone and come out on the brow of a sloping hill where there was grass and a wind blowing and one tall tree reaching into the infinite immensities of blueness. Quite suddenly, after a moment of quietness there, earth and sky and windblown grass and the child in the midst of them came alive together with a pulsing light of consciousness. There was a wild foxglove at the child's feet and a bee dozing about it, and to this day I remember the child looking everywhere for the source of this happy wonder, and at last she questioned–"God?"–because it was the only awesome word she knew. Deep inside, like the murmurous swing of a bell, she heard the answer, "God, God . . . "
>
> How long this ineffable moment lasted I never knew. It broke like a bubble at the sudden singing of a bird, and the wind blew and the world was the same again–only never *quite* the same.

To " . . . come alive together" is the sublime intimacy we all seek. Experiencing the fullness of being alive *and* together with everyone and everything *is* our home. It is where we know our-selves in the context of the whole, and know the whole to be our family. Living with the *knowing* makes us different from who we were before the Attentive Experience.

Feeling the fullness of "aliveness" is an experience of optimum health; for what is illness but a closing down of an organ or a system? Health is the opening, the full flowing of Life through us, whether we are speaking of the body or the psyche or the spirit.

Our busy, high technology, complex lives discourage the kind of experiences described. Our culture and our educational systems have pulled children away from their attentive experiences, ignored them or disdained them until the child has denied or repressed them. Adults who entertain such experiences are viewed as crazy (or saints, if they have been dead long enough). Clients have confided their experiences to me in hushed tones and embarrassed laughter, asking, "You won't tell anyone? I've never told that to anyone before." It is tragic that our precious glimpses into the mystical are hidden for fear of ridicule. Nevertheless whether one asks the child or the mystic, there is but one task and that is to pay attention. It may be called prayer, or meditation, or mindfulness, but the essen-tial element is the attentiveness. Attention is a compelling word that derives from the Latin "ad" meaning toward and "tenere" meaning to stretch. If we stretch our attention toward anything, a slug, a rainbow, oily water in a gutter, our breath, and hold it there, as does the small child, we can begin to know ourselves in our own fullness. If we take the time to do this regularly, we may soon find that we have developed an awareness that keeps us at One, Fully Alive. We will have become intimate with our world and with ourselves within our world. And we shall know "it is good."

The fruits of paying attention are many. We begin to know our-selves in an appreciative way. A child-like sense of wonder returns. We find ourselves filled with gratitude for all that is.

A Zen sesshin (a Buddhist retreat of silent meditation) that I made in the early seventies with Kennett-Roshi of the Mt. Shasta Abbey, impressed me with the power of gratitude. Having been spiritually conceived in the womb of Catholicism, I had the intel-lectual conviction that charity was the foundation of all virtue. Kennett-Roshi, using the metaphor of the lotus plant, explained that we were in the mud, growing our roots. Our root system is nourished with gratitude. We need not be concerned about being compassionate, for a grateful heart naturally overflows to others. I remember being struck with memories of the many "charitable acts" I had performed out of "duty" when I was tired and resentful. I was suddenly aware they had been merely self-serving "for my salvation." How grating they must have been for the recipients! On the other hand, how effortless it is to let one's abundance (for real abundance is gratitude) flow out to others. At those times one gives without being conscious of "giving" anything–one is simply "being." Kennett-Roshi went on to explain that compassionate action forms the stem of the lotus. If we continue to be grateful, with compassion flowing from the gratitude, wisdom will arise out of compassion to form the full bud. As wisdom grows, the bud fills out to blossom into enlightenment–all due to the grateful heart. It occurs to me that even as each one of us can be a lotus flower, all of us together are the One Lotus Flower. It is only as each of us practices being grateful in the mud of our lives that the One Lotus will bloom to unite us with a clarity and love that renders violence between us and our nations impossible.

Within our culture, perhaps the most telling result of a meaningful interior life is the personal power one gains. Internal power is the real power. Contrary to the old maxim "power corrupts," it is powerlessness that corrupts. It is true that people who gain positions of power can resort to physical might to enforce their authority, but this becomes necessary for them because they do not command the respect that comes from internal power. Those who have neither external nor internal power have only violence as their resort when their circumstances are seen as desperate. Dependency, which is the state of powerlessness, gives rise to hostility. Dependency activates our teenagers' anger to propel them out of the nest. It is why women leave husbands who are "masters." It is why any of us grit our teeth in frustration when we feel we are unable to make a difference in our national policies. Anger, unresolved, leads to violence. There are many approaches to dissipating anger. One can use energy demanding activities from chopping wood to aerobic sports, to beating mattresses, to structured fighting, to intensive breathwork. They are helpful to remove the body's acid that results from anger. They can melt the knot in the stomach. If the situation that caused the anger remains, the anger will return all too soon. Assertiveness is helpful to resolve situations, but there are those situations where even assertiveness fails. Nothing compares with internal power. With it one gains the confidence to assume "response-ability" (literally, the ability to respond) to assess the situation and to make the best choices possible. Assertiveness, as a technique, is not helpful unless there is confidence behind it. When one has assurance that one's personal convictions guide one's choices, one maintains his/her position with courage and hope and is not defeated internally. It is only when one feels helpless that one resorts to violence (either to him/her self or to others). *And violence is the plague of our nation.* Senator Hatfield (1991), contributing statistical information to the Congressional Record on the poverty and violence of our children, stated: ". . . "Everyday, 135,000 children take a gun to school. Every 32 seconds, a 15 to 19 year old woman becomes pregnant. Every 55 minutes a child is born to a mother who does not even hold a highschool diploma. And, finally, every 14 hours a child the age of five or younger is murdered." The unscrupulous management of the savings and loan institutions is a different form of violence, but violence nonetheless that robbed its investors of life savings. The American public is being required to pay thousands of dollars each (the amount continues to rise) to prevent the economic disaster the S&Ls' failures have threatened. Bill Moyers (1991), in a documentary of failed presidents, considered Reagan a failed president, despite all his popular successes: "The tragedy of the Reagan years is he assumed we really preferred the comfortable lie to the uncomfortable truth. He said we were standing tall when we were sliding back." Is this not another violent act?

There is a calm what comes with internal strength that frightens those who rely on physical might alone. I have a friend who marched up, armed with her kitchen apron, to a gang of young hoodlums swinging bicycle chains to terrorize the other children in the park, and quietly told them, as she looked the leader squarely in the eye, "You ought to be ashamed of yourselves." They stepped back from her steady gaze, dropped their chains and ran. I know a woman who faced a paranoid schizophrenic brandishing a knife, who disarmed him with only her internal calm (perhaps united with the eternal calm). Gorbachev faced the largest nuclear buildup in the world when he met with President Reagan and announced that he was going to do something terrible to him, he was going to deprive him of an enemy. And the Cold War began its thaw. We are all familiar with the power of the Buddha, the Christ, Ghandi, Martin Luther King, and many more. We tend to discount that power when it applies to ourselves, believing it to be the trait of the great. Each of us has access to our own internal strength, the strength that is one with all strength. It is that strength that dissipates our anger when we know we have the power to overcome violence. We no longer have cause to be angry. We know we shall not be victimized by anyone.

Whenever I review the problems of the couples I've seen in therapy, or when I observe the societal violence in our country, I come back to the basic need we have to develop our internal power. Our times demand that we value ourselves, understanding the divine within us, so we can be able to value others. Our society needs the childlike wonder and joy, the deep gratitude, the communion that we can enjoy together, if we but develop our inner life. Practicing mindfulness reaps high rewards with little cost.

The writings of Thich Nhat Hahn (1988, 1991), the Vietnamese Buddhist monk, and Brother David Steindl-Rast (1983, 1984), the Benedictine monk, are helpful supports for those who wish to follow attentive practices. The Native Americans introduce their young to them with the Vision Quest, a ritual for entrance into adulthood. If one is to find his/her home, one must get beyond *believing* in the One Love to *knowing* it in one's guts.

Modern psychology, traditionally, has chosen to disassociate itself from religion, identifying itself as a science. Its emphasis has been on rational theories supported by research and practiced by therapists guided by the theories and skilled in specific sets of techniques. It ignored spirituality which does not yield reproducible data. Interestingly, religion, in practice, has also distanced itself from mysticism by its rational, legalistic interpretations of the mystical message and its watering down of its rituals' mysteries. Ironically, hard science (the quantum physicists) is directing us back to the mystical with its theories of the "network of relationships" that underlie all physicality, the "one continuum." As is the network they posit, the ferment is everywhere. This is the Good News! It is gratifying to see the leading edge in psychology incorporating the spiritual: Jean Houston's *Therapeia* (1980, 1982, 1987), the transpersonal movement, the wholistic movement. Eugene Gendlin (1978) puts an emphasis on the sacred moment of connection with his focusing awareness. Ron Kurtz' Hakomi (Kurtz & Johanson, 1991) is a practice in mindfulness based on a trust in each person's inner wisdom. Virginia Satir's (1972, 1988) impact flowed from her generous heart giving its undivided attention to "the inner core" (Satir, 1988, pp. 340-341) of those she served. The "greats" in our profession (using various methodologies) are great because they care enough to be consistently attentive.

In a Seattle workshop sponsored by the Theosophical Society for caregiving professionals, Eric Peper, Ph.D. (1985), opened by acknowledging that, yes, we professionals do come together to increase our skill levels, but more importantly, underlying our skills is our *caring* level which we must also continually improve. So necessary is it that we find something we can genuinely care about, if only a potential that we see, in each and every person with whom we work, he warned, that if we dare to work with someone in whom we can find nothing likable, *we are guilty of malpractice!*

In short, we must love others as ourselves, because in fact, others are ourselves.

It is time for psychology to acknowledge that it is not viable without spirituality. It is time for the professionals in the field to acknowledge their attention to their own spirituality is a prerequisite for their effective work.

As therapists, it is important that we root out our hierarchal attitudes in order to foster equality. We do not "know better" than our clients. We can sometimes reflect others skillfully (as they often can with us, given the opportunity). We can explore together. We can grow together. When we learn simply "to be," we can then "be" with our clients. We have a basis for trusting their ability to do the same. We no longer need our clients to need us. We enter into our relationships with a sense of equality and sharing. Only then can we be confident that we are able to inspire. That is our work, to empower our clients. In Jean Houston's (1979) inimitable expression, "One's greatest genius is to prime the juice of another's potential."

The time has come to fill the spiritual void. The exciting news is that it is beginning to happen. Everywhere, mainline churches, New Age explorers, scientists, ordinary citizens, politicians, one senses the spiritual ferment among pockets of people. They are the leaven to which we can add our share, if we wish to see a moral integrity return to our nation. We can honestly make love . . . not war . . . in families, in nations. My wish for my newly married friends will then have a fertile field in which to come true.

REFERENCES

Austin, M. (1932). *Earth horizon.* Albuquerque: University of New Mexico Press.

Blake, W. (1964). Auguries of Innocence. In O. Williams (Ed.) *Major English poets* (p. 40) New York: Mentor.

Booth, L. (1991). When God Becomes a Drug. *Common Boundary, 9* (4) p. 28.

Census Bureau. (1991) *Statistical Abstracts of the United States.* III Ed. Washington, D.C.: U.S. Dept. of Commerce.

Fordham, F. (1953). *An introduction to Jung's psychology.* Baltimore, Md.: Penguin.

Gendlin, E. (1978). *Focusing.* New York: Everest House.

Greeley, A. (1991). First Word. *Omni Magazine, 13* (11).

Hatfield, M. (1991). *Congressional Record,* reported by *Parade Magazine.* August 14, 1991.

Houston, J. (1973). Notes from Jean Houston Workshop. University of California, Santa Cruz.

Houston, J. (1980). *Life-Force: the psycho-historical recovery of the self.* New York: Delacorte Press.

Houston, J. (1982). *The possible human.* Los Angeles: Jeremy P. Tarcher, Inc.

Houston, J. (1987). *Search for the beloved.* Los Angeles: Jeremy P. Tarcher, Inc.

Johanson, G., & Kurtz, R. (1991). *Grace unfolding: psychotherapy in the spirit of the Tao-te-Ching.* New York: Bell Tower, a Division of Crown Publishers.

Lederer, W. J., & Jackson, D. D. (1968). *The mirages of marriage.* New York: W. W. Norton.

Moyer, B. (1991). Bill Moyer Documentary. Reported by *Parade Magazine.* August 14, 1991.

Nhat Hanh, T. (1988). *The sun my heart.* Berkeley, CA.: Parallax Press.

Nhat Hanh, T. (1991). *Peace is every step.* New York: Bantam Books.

Schaef, A. W. (1986). *Co-Dependence.* Minneapolis: Winton press.

Schaef, A. W. (1987). *When society becomes an addict.* San Francisco: Harper & Row.

Steindl-Rast, D. (1983). *A listening heart: the art of contemplative living.* New York: Crossroad.

Steindl-Rast, D. (1984). *Gratefulness, the heart of prayer.* Ramsey, N.Y.: Paulist Press.

Response to Margaret Kirschner's Article: "There Is But One Love We Share"

Alma Silverthorn

I like this paper very much. It is well written, thoughtful and thought provoking.

I don't particularly like the idea that it is time for psychology to acknowledge that psychology is not viable without spirituality. I would foresee something awful coming out of that, given psychology's history. It would only be a short step to classification, codification, rigidity, and dogma. LO, we would have another *Religion* on our hands, probably with numerous denominations, schools, and gurus. I don't think psychology is equipped to fill the spiritual void.

Alma Silverthorn, PhD, member of editorial board of the *Journal of Couples Therapy,* is in private practice, Palo Alto, CA.

Blood and Oil

The war is over, and I'm told
we good guys won,
so God must love us,
and maybe that is why
he made so much sand—
to soak up all the blood
so we wouldn't leave a mess.
I'm trying to figure out
how much the war cost
and how many gallons
of blood were spilled,
and how much per gallon that comes to.
Probably a lot, and blood
doesn't even burn.
I never studied geology, so have to ask:
If we pump enough blood into the sand,
does it come back up as oil?

–Tom Greening

Tom Greening is Editor of the *Journal of Humanistic Psychology,* 1314 West-wood Boulevard, Los Angeles, CA 90024. "Blood and Oil" is from Greening's *Gulf War Poems* (1991) and is reprinted with permission. It appeared previously in "Special Reports," *Heartline* 3(2) 1991.

Mirror of Madness

Virginia O. Felder

SUMMARY. "Mirror of Madness" explores the yearning for revenge which paves the way for an addictive pattern of malicious behavior. The author uses stories from her own life and from her practice of psychotherapy to identify the "malice fix," an addictive response to pain which brings about momentary relief, yet, interferes with the possibility of genuine healing. The mirror of madness occurs as a distressed individual succeeds in getting someone else to exhibit pain and fury, reflecting these emotions back to the true source. The target person embodies the anguish, thereby relieving the initiator of the burden. The path of intervention into this relational dynamic is highlighted.

Malice has always fascinated me. My fascination comes from the pretense and illusion so often surrounding malice. They wrap it up giving it a different look; they cut off its real identity, preventing the possibility of a genuine response.

As is true with many people, my interests primarily grew out of my own experience. From the furthest depths of my memory, I was groomed to be a "killer." I recall the years of "sibling rivalry." My

---

Virginia Ovesen Felder, who received her Masters of Divinity and Masters of Theology in Pastoral Counseling from Columbia Theological Seminary, is a licensed Marriage and Family Therapist who has practiced psychotherapy since 1975. Currently, she is a clinical member of the American Academy of Psychotherapists and the American Association for Marriage and Family Therapists. She is Chairperson for the Atlanta Chapter of the Georgia Association for Marriage and Family Therapists, Past-President of the Biofeedback Society of Georgia, and of the Stone Mountain Ministerial Association, and author of numerous published articles on relationships. Correspondence may be addressed to Virginia O. Felder, 4262 Smithsonia Court, Tucker, GA 30084.

mother, early on, turned the emotional obligations and responsibilities of motherhood over to my sister, Mariann who was two and a half years older than I. My starvation for affection and my adoration of her resulted in my being a most obnoxious pest. The harder I fought for recognition and acceptance, the harder Mariann fought to maintain her space. Daily brawls became the norm in our struggle for survival. Verbal humiliation was the tongue most often spoken. I was a mean child. Hurt and angry, I drew motivation for living from my resentment and bitterness. My fury kept me alive.

I felt embarrassed about being mean, and yet, the only choices I knew were to be mean, or not be at all. I practiced becoming invisible, but it did not come naturally to me. I was much better at being outright hostile.

When I was a teenager, a shift took place. It happened one night, as my parents were going out, that Mother instructed me to use Mariann's alarm clock to get up in the morning. I had to be at school earlier than she did; so I could put it back in her room when I got up. When I explained this to Mariann, she refused to give me her clock, saying she did not believe Mother had told me to do that. After a few minutes of arguing, Mariann told me that if I would go and call Mother, and if she, indeed, said again that I was supposed to use her alarm clock, she would give it to me.

Well, even though I knew I would catch hell from Mother for bothering her with this ridiculous redundancy, I proceeded to jump the hoop. Having jumped, I returned to Mariann's room to find her door locked. As I beat on the door, I heard her yell, "I wouldn't let you in this room if you were Jesus Christ!" In that moment I experienced the "last straw," punctuating years of abuse. I no longer felt anxious or upset. I simply knew I was going to get the alarm clock or die trying. I did not much care which.

Our storage room housed most every tool imaginable. I managed to sufficiently disassemble the door to Mariann's room in order to get in. She was a bit surprised, but more outraged as she bounded off her bed at me. Scratching and pulling hair were usually adequate to turn me away . . . but not this time. We pushed and pulled, slapped and scraped for what seemed to be hours. We knocked into furniture and rolled around on the floor kicking and yelling. Finally, I grabbed a hair brush and hit her in the head as hard as I could. She promptly fell still. I stood up and looked at her. "Good!" I thought (consciously), while, at the same time, there was a part of me standing outside myself . . . horrified. The outside part mused, "You killed your sister, and you don't even care . . . " "No, I don't!" I answered in silence. I proceeded to unplug the alarm clock and take it to my room, locking the door behind me just in case she was not dead (which she wasn't). However, she never laid a hand on me in anger after that night.

So it was that I became a killer, one with a willingness to kill or be killed for the price of dignity. The identity fit. I was good at it. The only problem was that there was not much of a market for teenage killers. I channelled my energies into sports, basketball, softball, and running. The most satisfactory, by far, was tournament karate free-fighting competition . . . a great match! I could channel all these destructive energies into the fight, but people cheered and treated me like a heroine rather than a monster.

As years have passed, my inquisitiveness into malice has continued. Now, with a body too fragile for karate, my laboratory for experimentation has become the tennis court. It is the one place I allow myself to be shamelessly insensitive, impolite, cold and rude.

Recently, I was playing a league mixed doubles tennis match when I noticed that the gentleman, Jack, who was my opponent, was foot faulting. Normally, in these most polite social gatherings foot faults are never called. After the point was over, I said to him, "I just want to let you know that you are foot faulting, and if you do it again, I'm going to call it."

"You've got to be kidding; I can't believe you!" he scoffed.

"I've never heard of anyone calling a foot fault in this league," his partner scolded me. I thought it was interesting that her name was Mariann.

He served again. "Foot fault," I called loudly.

"This is ridiculous!" Jack bellowed. His serve was over. We changed courts in silence without any eye contact. I was aware of a distinct sense of delight with myself. I really enjoyed seeing Jack start to lose his cool. In the next game, I noticed that Jack quit trying to win points, and, instead, determined to take every opportunity to hit the ball as hard as he could . . . directly at me. Although I kept a stone face, inside, I was smiling. I love winning, and had been able to enlist Jack in helping my cause. Also, I had found myself in this situation often enough that I had gotten very good at ducking.

Before long, it was Jack's turn to serve again. His first serve was to me. I could not see his feet and watch the ball too. ("Oh darn!") On his next serve to my partner, I had a clear view to the baseline. He did it again. "Foot fault!" I called.

"This is the most ludicrous thing I've ever seen!"

"The rule states that you're supposed to stand behind the white line when you serve," I retorted condescendingly. I was exhilarated by the sense of power I felt. Jack backed up near the fence, about eight feet behind the baseline. He threw the ball up and hit it just as hard as he could. It stuck in the fence behind me.

"There, is that far enough back???!!" he screamed.

I wanted to say, "Hey, in case you haven't noticed, I can't watch your feet when you're serving to me. That really wasn't necessary, but you might try it again serving to my partner." However, I wasn't quite that tacky; besides, I didn't particularly want him to jump over the net and take a punch at me. But I was sure tickled with myself. I felt in total control.

He served to my partner, maybe hoping that his last antic would discourage my persistence by shaming me. "Foot fault," I called. That was it. He turned and just walked off the court in the middle of the match. I must admit, I was enjoying myself so much that I was a bit disappointed.

Later, as I reflected on the experience, I remembered something I had heard at a workshop on treating incest survivors. At the time, it struck me as being a very bold, and probably distorted, if not a totally false statement. The speaker asserted that, even though the research does not reflect it, she believed that 100% of all perpetrators of sexual abuse had been sexually abused.

My memories carried me back to the images in my mind as the speaker explained that the abuser watches the expression of confusion, terror, guilt, anguish, powerlessness and fury on the face of the victim and, in that moment, is freed from the burden of feeling those responses within him or herself. "What power there is in this sort of transfer," I thought.

In other, totally benign situations, I have seen this same dynamic. For instance, if my daughter is doing something that is dangerous, and my husband takes action to remove her from danger, I no longer feel the impetus to do anything. He carries that initiative I felt; and so, relieves me of the burden.

I thought back on the events of the tennis match. All of a sudden, I became aware that, as I watched Jack decompensate, he acted out all the emotions I had felt as a child: the frustration, the anger, the powerlessness. He momentarily relieved me of the burden of these emotions. I felt free from them. I realized that this was a big part of my elation, but it was only a temporary fix, like a decadent eating binge, or an alcoholic obliviousness. There was no real healing, nothing of lasting value . . . only the perpetuation of the wounds that had been passed on to me.

Another memory came to me. I once asked a wise woman how people could so clearly side with evil as to join a satanic cult. She pondered a moment, and then responded, "When one's experience is that the power of evil is greater than the power of good, he or she will side with evil in an effort to find security." I am aware that there is some element of evil in the destructiveness of my actions. In terms of power in competition, it has certainly been my experience that detaching from any compassion and embracing the "killer" part of myself is very effective in accomplishing the goal of winning. However, there is also something valuable in this experience besides just winning. Maintaining this ability to detach from others in order to stand for something, something worth living for, something worth dying for, allows me to move through life with some confidence in confronting any challenge. Certainly, tennis matches have nothing to do with these elements essential to real living, yet they serve as an arena to hone the emotional skills of warfare.

I have long appreciated the treasures of these experiences in terms of maintaining my inner strength; but this particular tennis match was the first time I realized how unconsciously connected I was to my victim. I remember a friend of mine making the comment that all anger is dependent. Dependent . . . that's one attribute I don't like to claim. Only now do I see just how utterly dependent this type of experience is.

I began reflecting on my intimate relationships. I recognize that in marriage there is a tendency to do the same kind of transferring of feelings onto a spouse. If I can get my husband to be irritable with a slow waiter, I don't feel a bit bothered by the wait. More directly, if I can find a blemish in my partner that gives me occasion to criticize and denigrate, the angry reactions churned up in him relieve me of those feelings in myself.

In working with couples, I have often wondered what the pay-off was for those who stay embroiled in competition for moral righteousness. I remember a consultation I did with a couple who had been married forty-two years. Each spouse had absolutely nothing to say about the other except what was wrong with him or her. And, although both people said they really wanted to change the way they went about relating to each other, each insisted that the other person must change first.

I shared the following story with the couple. I married a man whose mother was a home-ec teacher. He knew everything about how a home was supposed to be kept, and he very willingly imparted this information along to me. One day, early in our marriage, I decided I wanted to create a wonderful surprise for him. I secretly took a day off work and stayed home cleaning our apartment from top to bottom, just the way I envisioned his mother would.

He walked in from work that evening and promptly exclaimed, "You left the damn faucet dripping again!" The couple did not seem to catch the meaning of the story which seemed obvious to me; so I decided to just let them sit with it.

I have long known that there is no way to do things so well or be so good that we are invulnerable to criticism, but only now do I recognize the important role this emotional sparring plays in enabling the addiction of the "malice fix." We can use our spouse to numb us out so that we do not feel our own wounds. The degree of pain from our own wounds determines the frequency and intensity of the fix we need. Our partner becomes the mirror into which we reflect our madness in hopes of ridding our soul of the burden.

The most devastating aspect of this pattern is that, not only is the "fix" temporary, it is impossible for real healing to occur until one quits relying on the addiction to bring relief. Until I recognize the remnants of pain still hurting in me and accept them as my responsibility to address, lasting healing will not occur.

I have been struck by the determination of families who are involved in capital offense cases to bring the perpetrator to the fullest sentence possible. This course of action often takes over ten years. During this time, the family must maintain the freshness of their pain in order to convince any jury of the devastation of the crime. It is only once a final appeal has been made that the family members can get on with the business of working through their grief. They seek to create a mirror in the accused so that they can see reflected the torment they have felt themselves.

As a society, we teach people to use this mirror as a fix on every level, from dyadic relationships on up to national wars. When this dynamic is blessed by a group of people, it gains power and momentum in its potential destructiveness. Individuals within the group tend to respond to a "herd consciousness" without questioning the wisdom behind decisions made and without awareness of any responsibility for the pain inflicted. The exhilaration of victory (seeing the pain embodied in an "other") masks the aches within our own national soul.

In playing tennis, there have been a few people who have not responded to the invitation I extended to enter into this addictive agreement. One couple we played was genuinely playful and gentle with each other as well as with my partner and me. This stance, of course, represents a particular kind of challenge to me. I was a total jerk in every way I could imagine that might ruffle their feathers. In a pause between sets, the woman asked my partner, with authentic concern, "Is she having any fun?"

My partner simply responded, "Oh yeah, she's just real intense; that's her way of having fun."

Then the woman said, "Oh, that's good." [I hate playing well-adjusted people. It's so much more difficult when I cannot get them to play against themselves!] They succeeded, as a few others have, to get through the entire match simply having fun.

In observing couples, I find that those individuals who either did not experience significant abuse growing up, or who have done the work necessary to heal their inner wounds, are far less likely to respond to invitations to self-destructiveness in order to accommodate someone else's need for a fix. However, everyone, no matter how healthy he or she may be, certainly experiences the inner reaction of wanting to strike out and inflict pain on someone who is hurting them. It works hand-in-hand with the fight-or-flight response of the autonomic nervous system. At some point in the evolution of humanity, it was probably very functional, but I would suggest that, at this juncture in history, its usefulness has been outworn, and it has become more of a liability to human relatedness than a necessary tool for survival. It is time to expose the true nature of the mirror and what is really reflected.

Making Meaning:
Living in a Both/And World

Penny Cupp

The theme of this volume intrigued me. I came of age in the 60s, so the first part, "Make Love, Not War," brings back memories not only of experiences around the Viet Nam era, but also of the youthful energy and optimism about social and political systems, as well as personal relationships. Love was all we needed. The afterthought, " . . . Or at Least Make Meaning," is reflective of the more mature position in which I find myself now as a person and as a psychotherapist. I believe that we can use whatever happens in our lives for growth and deeper understanding of ourselves if we can make meaning of the conflict and chaos in which our lives become entangled. So whether we make love or make war, we need to make meaning of our lives: our decisions, actions, feelings, needs, goals.

Our need to make meaning is related to our need to see ourselves in control of our lives and our destinies. If one feels in control of life events, one is less likely to experience negative effects on health and life satisfaction (Matheny & Cupp, 1983). This principle led me to work with people to help them gain a greater sense of control over their lives. To accomplish that end in working with couples, I use a model that teaches them to recognize their own needs, ask for what they want, and negotiate differences. This approach focused on the sense of control within the relationship. I also recognize, however, that in the larger world there are random events that impact the lives of individuals over which there is no possibility of

Penny Cupp, PhD, is in private practice at 5180 Roswell Road, NW, Suite 201 N, Atlanta, GA 30342.

control. War is one of those events. In order to avoid the deleterious effects of such events, the individual or the couple must have some way of making meaning of these events which allows a sense of control, at least of the outcomes, so that the person has a sense of control of his or her own destiny. I believe that one's ability to create meaning in the face of chaotic events is enhanced by a strong primary bond with another human being; thus, being in a healthy couple's relationship creates something of a buffer against the stress of the outer world (Cupp, 1985).

I have debated about whether to address this issue on the more microscopic level of the couple, the dyadic unit wherein we make both love and war in our search for fulfillment, or on the more literal and global level concerning the effects of war on the couple as the basic dyadic component and building block of society. I would like to address both because I have personal experience with both. Perhaps if we could learn to love each other better at the dyadic level, we would have more harmony and cooperation at the global level.

LIVING IN AN "EITHER/OR" WORLD

Most of us have been reared in an "either/or" world. We have been presented with dichotomies such as "Make Love, Not War." One is taught to see the world in terms of good or evil, male or female, right or wrong, love or war. What has happened to the "both/and"? Do we not live in a world where the reality is that there is good and evil, male and female, right and wrong, love and war? More and more I try to avoid the "either/or" dilemma. I look for ways, in my life and in my therapy, to create a "both/and" world. I want to avoid dichotomies: the breaking down of situations into opposite and mutually exclusive choices. Couples often come to therapy believing there is an either/or choice: stay or leave. They come hoping for some change (usually in the partner) or revelation that will make the choice clear. I work with couples to create, instead, a world where the ruling principle is not a dichotomy but rather a synergy, where the focus is on "building up" instead of "tearing down," a world in which conflict or competition does not divide or reduce us, but where there is expansion, building up, creating more than was before. Couples who adopt a "both/and" world view are more likely to respect each other's differences and they have increased options for conflict resolution.

Karen Horney (1937) talked about three forms of interpersonal interaction: moving toward, moving away from and moving against. Love is generally seen as "moving toward." War is "moving against." "Moving away from" is disengagement. Both love and war are forms of engagement. But it need not be, it cannot be, an "either/or" choice. In any human relationship both love and war, connection and conflict, have a place in the context of the larger meaning of the relationship. This is reflected in philosophy in the Hegelian Dialectic: there is Thesis, Antithesis, and Synthesis. That is, there is the current state of affairs (Thesis), the oppositional or renewing forces (Antithesis), and the resultant growth toward a higher order (Synthesis). Without conflict, love is stagnant, the "happily-ever-after" ending of fairy tales.

Ideally the relationship of a couple, the primary pair bond, should be to create an atmosphere of acceptance and safety which enables each person to experience himself or herself authentically and to move toward self-actualization, to move from the "what is" to the "what could be." Judith Bardwick (1979) posits the need for "existential anchoring" in the context of the primary relationship in order to free each person to explore and fully develop his or her own identity. In a primary relationship, we may appear at times to be adversaries, but we are also, and more truly, allies. We work to maximize each other's welfare and growth, emphasizing the need to make love, to make our relationships more loving, and to understand the meaning of conflict as it engenders growth.

MAKING LOVE

I fear that we live in a culture which has not taught us adequately about how to love. Our language of love is impoverished. The Eskimos purportedly have something like seventeen words for snow to describe its subtle variations because it is so important for their survival. I think we need at least seventeen words for love. We use the word to mean so many things. We need more precision if we are to find meaning.

Our need to learn more about love impacts on many levels: it's like a series of concentric circles. Beginning with loving ourselves, we learn more about loving as a couple. That, in turn, impacts on our ability to love as a family, to express love within our community, our country, and our world. It moves from the personal to the global.

So let me begin with the personal. I feel like I have had two very different lives in the last twenty-five years. For twenty of those years I was the wife of a career Army officer. We married in the sixties. I was torn between my own focus on "making love," on being a pacifist and a humanist, and my admiration and respect for the patriotism, love of country, and devotion to ideals that I saw in my husband as he accepted the inevitability of his service in the war in Viet Nam. Both of our fathers had served in World War II, the honorable thing to have done. His father continued in a military career which spanned 34 years. The way we both made meaning of Lloyd's military career was to view it as a necessity for the preservation of the American way of life. His job was to protect democracy and my job was to support him in this pursuit.

Then something rather unexpected happened along the way. I became a psychotherapist. I began graduate school in the waning years of Lloyd's military career. He made dramatic sacrifices in his career to accommodate the needs of my growing aspirations. While on the surface this may seem like an "either/or" choice, I believe it was a move toward creating a "both/and" world for us as a couple. I attribute part of his willingness to do this to our experience with Marriage Encounter, which taught Lloyd to value his feelings and the importance of our dyadic connection. We wanted our marriage to support the optimal growth for each of us as individuals as it supported us growing into the maturity of our relationship. This goal could not be achieved through the domination of one over the other. Instead we learned a kind of cooperation in which we have played leap-frog with our lives, so that the growth of one supersedes, then supports, the growth of the other. When it became apparent that I was serious about my career, Lloyd volunteered for a short tour in Korea (meaning a separation of one year) so that I could continue in my doctoral program. When he retired from active duty, I became the main support for the family so that he could return to school to retrain for a second career in teaching and coaching, which was what he truly wanted to do. On the dyadic level, loving each other meant making sacrifices that served both self and the other. It was cooperation rather than competition that saw us through. Each of us supported the optimal growth of the other in areas that gave meaning to our personal lives and to our lives together. This was one way of making love and making meaning.

MAKING WAR

At the same time we were impacted with the necessity of "Making War," both on the global and personal levels. On the global level, Lloyd was a career soldier, committed to making war in the service of higher ideals. His tour in Viet Nam had a potentially devastating impact on our personal relationship. Having a spouse who goes to war has an impact of both building bridges and building walls within a relationship. It builds bridges in the sense that we assume that we are both dedicated and supportive of the reasons he goes to war. We believe in the political structures of our country and the need to protect our way of life. But the impact of the reality of his going to war was something else: the reality was more a building of walls. While I believed that, as an adult, I should understand the need for the higher good of the society, on a personal level I felt abandoned, scared, lonely, inadequate to cope with all that had been left to me. This contrast of the political ideal and the reality at the societal level parallels the contrast of idealism and reality within the couples' relationship. We had married young. I had expected that my husband would protect and take care of me. Then I found myself, at the age of twenty-three, with a small child, all on my own. We had married with the romantic myth of mutual dependency. We would take care of each other. But where was he now? He was tending to the defense of democracy; I was faced with the daily needs of myself and our son. His care-taking was at a global level; mine was very personal. Neither of us could really take care of the other. The myth offered us no guidance at this point. The walls that were built were our mutual need to protect the other. He minimized the horrors of war and I minimized the trials of single parenthood and feeling alone and unsupported in the world. We protected each other, but we denied each other the intimacy of our shared neediness. We protected each other from demands which we felt the other could not understand or meet. And so the walls grew. We moved from the myth of mutual dependence to the reality of independence, convincing each other of our ability to operate without the other.

At the end of the conflict and separation, we had to learn to let each other in again. At first we brought the conflict of the war into our relationship. We were each jealously protecting our own turf; we fought a lot in the first few months after Lloyd returned from Viet Nam, and our fighting was loud and dirty. We were angry that the myth of mutual dependency had let us down and we blamed each other. It was scary to trust again and difficult to give up the control each of us had created as a form of protection. Intimacy only happens when there is a surrender of that control, and one of the rules of war is "never surrender."

I was able to use the experience of being a waiting wife during Viet Nam as I worked with the dependents of soldiers mobilized for Desert Storm in 1991. I could understand their fear and their loneliness. I urged them to use the various support networks available to them and to keep the lines of communication open with their partners, sharing the good and the bad news, the positive and the negative feelings. I warned them to expect some profound changes in themselves and in their partners.

I also use my experience of the more internal, personal wars in all my work with couples (Cupp, 1991). War is generally a struggle for power and domination. As a couples' therapist, I am constantly aware of the impact of "making war" within the dyadic relationship. The mythic ideal in our culture is that when you are in love there is no conflict. But the reality, which may seem paradoxical, is that in the absence of conflict there can be no real intimacy. Intimacy requires that each person be him or herself; conflict is inevitable. I agree with Hendrix' Imago theory (1988) which suggests that we unconsciously choose partners who will invite us to grow by re-creating the psychodynamic conflicts of our early developmental years. Thus conflict is inherent in the deepest meaning and purpose of the primary relationship. The true art of intimacy is the willingness to face the conflict, to be different and to be accepted in that difference. Intimacy is the willingness to work through the differences and to find a common ground.

FINITE VERSUS INFINITE GAMES

In a very provocative book, Carse (1986) discusses finite versus infinite games. Finite games have rules and a clear winner; they are played for the goal of winning. Infinite games make room for creativity, spontaneity, and are played for the goal of continuing the game. War is a finite game, whether played on the battlefields of the world or the battlefields of the bedroom. It is a power struggle wherein the winner is also a loser; in winning one loses the possibility of intimacy and growth. Winning means domination and eliminates the possibility of a relationship of equals. But even in the finite games of war at the global level, we are devastated by losing an opponent with whom to play. What do we do after the war? We give money and other forms of support to re-build our opponent in order that they gain the strength to play again. It is impossible to play alone. To annihilate each other is to end the game. At the dyadic level, the movie "The War of the Roses" makes this point quite clearly.

I believe that the hope for making meaning out of our dyadic wars is to engage in an infinite game, in which the goal is to continue the play. The reality of the dynamic couples' relationship is not dependence or independence, but interdependence. If we are to bring passion to our love-making, there will also be times of conflict, times of making war. We are only willing to fight for those things about which we truly care. But our domestic wars must not be focused on annihilation of the other; without him or her the game cannot continue. Perhaps the ultimate question is "What is the meaning of our lives, as individuals and as couples?" I believe the answer is the self actualization of each person, which promotes the evolution of society as a whole. Furthermore, I believe we do that more fully in relationship than in isolation. In the healthiest sense, making love is supporting each other to grow into all we can be;

making war is challenging each other into this growth. But in order for the war to make meaning there must be a sense of supporting the other in the ability to continue to play out the game; for it is only in having a worthy opponent, in having a partner of equal strength and ability, that we are able to test and extend our own strength and ability to live life fully and to discover and express all that we truly are.

REFERENCES

Bardwick, J. M. (1979). *In transition*. New York: Holt, Rinehart and Winston.

Carse, J. P. (1986). *Finite and infinite games*. New York: Ballantine Books.

Cupp, P. (1985). *Prediction of illness based on life stress and coping resources: A study of sex differences*. Unpublished doctoral dissertation, Georgia State University, Atlanta, Georgia.

Cupp, P. (1991). They also serve who only stand and wait. *Voices, 27*, 93-104.

Hendrix, H. (1988). *Getting the love you want*. New York: Henry Holt, Publishers.

Horney, K. (1937). *The neurotic personality of our time*. New York: W. W. Norton and Company.

Matheny, K. B. & Cupp, P. (1983). Control, desirability, and anticipation as moderating variables between life change and illness. *Journal of Human Stress, 9*, 14-23.

Dilemmas of Difference:
Differentiating Couples Therapy Issues
for Intervention, Negotiation,
Separation or Celebration

Petruska Clarkson

SUMMARY. This paper outlines a particular conceptual framework or working tool which individuals, couples and couples therapists have found useful in exploring the meaning of love and separateness, increasing the opportunities for love in couples relationships and reducing the potential for war in the intimacy zone. Three categories of difference between partners are outlined as an example both of specific couples therapy work in the microcosm, and of the relationships of nations in the macrocosm.

INTRODUCTION

The ideas in this paper are designed to evoke questioning of what the therapist can and cannot hope to facilitate, and what the couple

Petruska Clarkson, MA, PhD, Associate Fellow of the British Psychological Society, is a chartered clinical psychologist, a practicing psychotherapist, supervisor, trainer and OD consultant. She is a member of the British Psychological Society's Counselling Section and Clinical Psychology Division, Chairperson of the Gestalt Training Institute of Great Britain, President for the British Institute for Integrative Psychotherapy, and a Teaching Member of the International Transactional Analysis Association (I.T.A.A.). She is the Principal Clinical Psychologist and a founder director of *metanoia* Psychotherapy Training Institute, 13 North Common Road, London W5 2QB, England which, among other programmes, runs training and supervision in Integrative Couples Therapy. She is the author of articles and books on psychotherapy, the most recent being *Transactional Analysis Psychotherapy: An Integrated Approach* (1992), London: Routledge.

75

realistically can or cannot hope to achieve, in couples counseling or therapy. Exploring the feasibility or likelihood of effective therapeutic action towards different therapeutic goals can sometimes prevent disillusionment and despair. Clarifying the kind of goals and achievability or morality of certain desired changes in couplehood seems to me vitally important, and sometimes a neglected aspect of couples work. Disagreement about the categories of difference I put forward here is to be welcomed and explored between the partners and the therapist. Such disagreement can be used to enrich the viability and usefulness of this contribution to the resources of the couples therapist.

It has been my experience in doing couples work, including training and supervising, that by sorting such desired changes into different categories, all parties can focus on more realistically achievable goals. Thus they can potentially reach greater satisfaction. It is therefore an attempt to put into couples work the spirit of the famous prayer usually attributed to St. Francis of Assisi:

> God, grant me the serenity to accept the things I cannot
>   change;
> The courage to change the things I can;
> And the wisdom to know the difference.

In order to deepen my understanding of my work with couples, my personal journey, and my experiences of organizations, I have found it useful to study macrosystems such as nations in the processes of change. Often the large systems reflect similar processes to the smaller ones and the microsystems reflect learning about the macrosystems. Nations are the large-scale experiments in humans living together where good outcomes lead to peace, harmony and creativity. As with couples, however, misunderstandings about differences between peoples can also explode into war.

THREE CATEGORIES OF DIFFERENCE

I wish to draw out some patterns currently apparent to me which apply both to couples and nations. This is done in the knowledge that I cannot, and am not attempting to, do justice to the full complexity of a matter which has preoccupied the human race since the dawn of time, and will continue to do so ad infinitum. For the moment I am separating out three categories of problem. These categories of difference can be termed *Unacceptable Behavior, Negotiable Issues,* and *Unchangeable Aspects of Self.* I think that they apply usefully in doing work with couples and may also apply usefully in mediation with groups, organizations, and larger systems such as nations.

Unacceptable Behavior

The first category of difference between partners concerns areas of unacceptable behaviors. In other words: "This is what I won't accept from you." It is behavior of the other person or other party which is essentially non-negotiable and in an ultimate moral sense shouldn't be up for negotiation. This concerns the basic human needs for security, economic well-being, a sense of belonging, recognition, and control over one's own life (Fisher & Ury, 1981/1983, p. 50). Whenever any of these needs are threatened, absent, or denied, effective reconciliation or mediation work is substantially impeded, if not impossible, because one cannot meaningfully negotiate between a torturer and a victim until the victim is at least on an equal footing with the torturer. Any such *"negotiation"* is an attempt to escape victimhood, not to exchange value. Such cases are not genuine transactions between equal human beings, both of whom deserve respect.

A woman's economic well-being is totally at the mercy of a vengeful and vindictive husband when he deprives her of either information or influence about how even her own earned income is spent. In couples therapy they cannot be said to be in a negotiating position on an equal basis. Where basic human needs are not honored, war or war-like actions follow almost inevitably.

> Negotiations are not likely to make much progress as long as one side believes that the fulfillment of their basic human needs is being threatened by the other. In negotiations between the United States and Mexico, the US wanted a low price for

Mexican natural gas. Assuming that this was a negotiation over money, the US Secretary of Energy refused to approve a price increase negotiated with the Mexicans by a US oil consortium. Since the Mexicans had no other potential buyer at the time, he assumed that they would then lower their asking price. But the Mexicans had a strong interest not only in getting a good price for their gas but also in being treated with respect and a sense of equality. The US action seemed like one more attempt to bully Mexico; it produced enormous anger. Rather than sell their gas, the Mexican government began to burn it off, and any chance of agreement on a lower price became politically impossible. (Fisher & Ury, 1981/1983, p. 50-51)

Domination (for example, when a wife is overruled through superior financial or physical strength of her partner), violence, a threat to the person or to their property, disenfranchizement (for example, when blacks are deprived of their right to vote in South Africa), all mean that the possibility for effective therapy or resolution is drastically reduced, if not made impossible.

I had an initial consultation with a couple where the man was quite a high-ranking member of the professional community. The wife pleaded with him to come to couples therapy with me because he frequently threatened her and on more than one occasion had pushed her around or even hit her. She was frightened by his behavior and yet unwilling or unable to call for help. Because of his standing in the community and his public reputation for being kind and generous she hoped that this could be resolved in couples therapy. He was, however, completely unwilling to accept personal responsibility for his threats of violence, for the terrorizing nature of driving fast and recklessly with her as a passenger when he was angry with her, for throwing large objects in her direction when he felt aggravated with her, or for engaging in acts of self-mutilation such as head banging, or breaking objects.

Naturally, this was very frightening to her and although she loved him, she could find no way to control him in such explosive rages. During these times he believed that she was accusing him of being mad or bad. The only way that she could escape from the verbal and threatened abuse was to leave the scene. Yet her love and concern for him seemed to rivet her to the interaction. She was trying to relieve his distress and of course deal with her own terror. He merely experienced it as further provocation and an incitement to more and more psychotic behavior.

At their initial consultation I asked him if he was willing to agree not to be violent or to threaten violence with her again. His statement was "Of course I can do that–unless she provokes me." What constitutes provocation in situations where one person is at the mercy of another physically or financially, is open to a great deal of interpretation. Victims are often kept in this position by the abuser telling them that they are paranoid, oversensitive, or lying (Dorfman, 1992). The secrecy that surrounds marital or physical and sexual child abuse makes it notoriously hard for the child or the injured spouse to be believed. Yet we now know that this is one of the most potent acts of healing to begin a journey back to personal empowerment (Miller, 1985 and 1979/1987). Blaming victims for their abuse at the hands of others is a collectively well-documented phenomenon, in the same way that children can be blamed or blame themselves for the fact that they were party to abusive situations (Caplan, 1985). A prisoner who refuses half rations of food, or objects to inhuman conditions, is often considered a troublemaker and a provocateur, only to be punished more violently if he or she complains of such treatment (Makhoere, 1988).

I asked the woman whether she was willing to call in the police next time he terrorized her. She was unwilling to do this knowing that he had a psychiatric history. Confronted with his unwillingness to offer his wife a basic sense of security, I refused to work with them as a couple. This was not only because it was an emotional victim/persecutor situation, but because she was actually in danger if he was so unwilling or unable to accept responsibility for his own violence. Her justifiable distress was exacerbated because of her loving concern not to expose his secret brutality at the expense of his professional reputation.

So any form of fascism where one person of a couple is enforcing through physical, financial, or emotional violence or threats of violence, the compliance of the other person constitutes for me an area of unacceptable, non-negotiable behavior. I do not think that couples work is appropriate at this level in many cases. What is more appropriate is to separate out the abused spouse/partner until he or she has reclaimed his or her basic human rights and can feel emotionally and financially like an equal human being. This is often impossible while they are still in a mutually self-reinforcing abusive system. Only when their basic human rights have been protected can threatened or abused individuals genuinely go into the arena of reclaiming their emotional and psychological equality.

Extreme cases, such as the ones mentioned above, are quite easy to recognize. Couples work where one gets habitually drunk and aggressive, whether it be on alcohol or jealousy, is notoriously difficult unless the co-dependency of the partner and their covert consent to their partner's brutality is withdrawn. Often separate work with each of the partners is indicated (Dryden, 1985). There are less extreme examples of unacceptable behaviors which, I believe, must be articulated between couples, usually in the beginning stages of their relationship, if it is not to lead to explosive or embittered breakdowns later. Ideally, these pre-requirements would be discussed early on in the relationship so that each partner understood as clearly as possible what the other partner considered to be absolutely non-negotiable, or beyond the pale, ground for breakdown, and unforgivable.

People differ surprisingly as to what they consider to be unacceptable. For one person it may be lying (by commission or omission), for another it may be infidelity, for another it may be financial betrayal. This area is different for different people, and is often not the same for both partners in a couple. One may find casual sex forgivable but not a genuine, loving relationship with another person outside of the couple (whether platonic or otherwise). One person may find it easy to live with somebody who is unreliable and unpredictable about time or keeping their promises. For another person, violations of such contracts would constitute grounds for irreparable breakdown. Having unprotected sex with another person has now entered the unacceptable area for most couples, whereas invasion of privacy, such as reading your partner's diary, or going through their private papers, might not be considered so unforgivable by some.

It is important to note that sometimes one spouse in a couple may accept the violation of their bodies, dignity, or autonomy early on in the relationship. They may even welcome or collude with abusive behavior, particularly if it is secret and confined to the privacy of the bedroom. However, when the abused spouse, for example, goes into psychotherapy and begins to experience and assert his or her basic human rights to freedom from physical threat and financial influence over their own lives, the other partner may experience this as extremely disturbing. The partner who is threatened with loss of control over the other may escalate threatening or abusive behavior. It may seem to them as if the original psychological level contract between them is failing. Their request to "Be the person that I married"–i.e., stop changing and becoming autonomous, is often based on fear of the threat of change, and a desperate wish to defend the rightness of precedent–however unfair it was.

The kind of couples therapy required in this category of difference is obviously radically different from that required for issues potentially harmful to life or property such as miscommunication, sexual adjustment, and differences about parenting. In extreme situations what is most important and most required may be education as to basic human freedoms, prisoners' rights, legal or police protection, refuges, and so on.

Sometimes what is unacceptable to one partner is not concerned with a basic human right but is particular to their history, or their individual sensibilities. Veronica was sexually abused while being almost strangled as a child. When her breathing is restricted during lovemaking she gets very anxious. I believe that this kind of difference should not be labeled pathological because she finds it unacceptable. Whether or not the person has been traumatized in a particular fashion, an equal and respectful relationship must be based on concern and consideration for each other's psychological lesions (Berne, 1980), belt lines (Bach & Goldberg, 1974/1983), and fears, whether or not they seem understandable or "reasonable" to the partner.

If something falls into the category of unacceptable behavior, we are discussing the pre-requisites for establishing a relationship, or the ground conditions for continuing a relationship; for example, "I will not stay with you if you continue drinking." It is, therefore, more figural and emphasized towards the beginning or ending of relationships. If these issues are not resolved further, couples work may even cause damage. For example, continuing to work in couples therapy on communication styles when a woman's life or economic freedom is endangered does not constitute good psychology. People are not free to take emotional risks, or to grow and develop in partnership, when their basic rights are threatened or denied. We are thus talking here about the essential pre-conditions for effective couples counseling; or to put it another way, if these issues are not resolved then the therapist may be colluding with cruelty or injustice at some level, since to remain neutral is to favor the aggressor in many such cases. Continuing without an agreed foundation, or with a wrongly assumed foundation to the relationship may also cause damage; and this is to be found both in the microcosm of couples relationships and also in the macrocosm of inter-racial and international issues, such as the current situation in South Africa.

I have been a voluntary exile from South Africa since after 1976 when black schoolchildren were being killed in increasing numbers for protesting against the injustices of the South African Bantu education system. Many black people rebelled against the infamous apartheid laws which attempted conformity by forcing them to be educated in a language not their own. They also rightfully resisted the attempt to make cultural and skin color differences the basis for their oppression and disenfranchizement. After the release of Mandela and the lifting of the state of emergency in 1990 I returned to work and to learn for a short while in the country of my birth. The heritage of injustice, cruelty and abuse over generations remains appalling. Recent changes are only somewhat ameliorating and do not reach to the heart of the abuses perpetrated over centuries. Notwithstanding appearances, people are still being tortured, still disenfranchised, still discriminated against. Yet, I found that the hope of change for the better is still possible as long as we can retain our empathy for others as human beings.

Unbelievably . . . there is an astonishing level of compassion, love and tolerance still left. They call it UBUNTU—which means fellow human feeling—and it is because of this that she still feels tremendous hope that the horrendous problems that are South Africa can progress towards peace. (Clarkson, 1990, p. 11)

It is important to separate non-negotiable from negotiable areas of work in couples therapy. It should not be negotiable to be treated with respect as a human being–to experience Ubuntu or fellow-feeling. Even criminals or prisoners of war are protected by law from cruel and unjust treatment, and no matter what provocative thing a spouse may *say*, nothing within our legal or moral system should justify acts of violence and cruelty in response. When these non-negotiable areas are no longer in dispute, the abusing spouse can be relied upon both to cease his or her abusive behavior, and the abused spouse can be relied upon to protect him- or herself. Mutual respect becomes the foundation for dealing with issues which can be negotiated between two equal human beings.

Negotiable Issues

The next category concerns those issues which are essentially negotiable between a couple. This is the area where most couples work of an understanding, improving, reconciling, and transformative nature can take place. Once a couple are clear about what is and what is not acceptable as pre-requirements, or what would constitute grounds for an irretrievable breakdown, then they can begin to deal with the differences in attitudes and behaviors which they can, and may be willing to change. It is helpful if these are concerned with those aspects of attitude and behavior which are genuinely changeable. It concerns the area of: "This is what I do or don't want you to do, and this is what you do or don't want me to do."

This is the area where the relationship can be worked–where it becomes a yoga for individual development and interpersonal bonding. We have *chosen* specific people to be our partners, and in that sense they can bring us some of the most significant developmental opportunities that can ever come our way. It is in this most intimate relationship with another person that we can get to know ourselves most truly, and risk knowing another most profoundly. It is in this space between two people that new life and new meaning can arise. From such an alchemical marriage a philosopher's stone of great wisdom, compassion, and transformative potential can be formed. I have often called life the great co-therapist because it brings so many opportunities to my clients and myself, often at exactly the most critically sensitive periods, to develop, change, transform, or abandon aspects of my self, defences, potential, or my capacity for intimacy. In this way our partners bring us, I think perhaps even in a karmic sense, specific existential opportunities for healing and creative evolution (Clarkson, 1991).

Most couples therapy literature concerns issues in this category of negotiable changes (Gellert, 1983; Satir, 1967/1978). For the purposes of this paper I would like to draw attention to selected specific issues. It is frequently said that marriage is a case of give and take. It may be a fallacy, though, that both people need to give or take the same kind of things. If one person in the couple likes sitting in the front row at the theater and the other in the second row, it can be a simple matter in an equal relationship to take turns, one time both sitting in the front row, the next time both sitting in the second row. Preferences for sexual activities, providing they are not in the unacceptable area for either, can be swapped, exchanged, or even traded in similar way: "Tonight I'll scratch your back for you because you really like it, and tomorrow night you'll brush my hair for me because I really like that."

One of the most frequently occurring misunderstandings which I encounter in the area of change-able attitudes and behaviors in couples work is the erroneous belief that my partner likes or should like what I like, or dislike what I dislike. One of the commonest and most prevalent sources for misunderstanding is the human inclination to give others what *we* want rather than to give them what they want. In the simplest terms, Mary likes to be hugged and cuddled and taken to bed when she's upset, and Jim likes to be distracted and taken out for a meal or a movie. When Jim finds Mary upset, he takes her out to distract her and finds it difficult to understand why she is not delighted with his attempts to amuse and entertain her. On the other hand, when Jim is upset, Mary feels puzzled and alienated when he does not respond to her nurturing and caretaking offers to put him to bed and bring him dinner there. The variations of misunderstandings on this theme are too numerous to contemplate. "I like surprise parties therefore I'll give you one," not thinking (or believing) that you can be so different from me that you hate them (even though you've told me this before!).

> Consider . . . the two sisters quarreling over an orange. Each sister wanted the orange, so they split it, failing to realize that one wanted only the fruit to eat and the other only the peel for baking. In this case as in many others, a satisfactory agreement is made possible because each side wants *different* things. This is genuinely startling if you think about it. People generally assume that differences between two parties create the problem. Yet differences can also lead to a solution. (Fisher & Ury, 1981/1983, p. 76)

This may also apply to helping each other solve problems. Mary does not want Jim to give her solutions until she has had time to explore her feelings, and cry and rage if she wants to. It is helpful to her if Jim shows her empathy and unconditional acceptance while she explores her own feelings and options, but she enjoys coming to her own solutions. Jim has a different style of problem-solving. He likes being given advice or quick-fire solutions as soon as he has stated his problem, and finds talking about it and exploring his emotions frequently a waste of time. When Mary comes home with a problem, he bombards her with solutions, and when Jim comes home with a problem, Mary withholds all suggestions and fruitlessly encourages him to find solutions.

The biggest confusion seems to be a common distortion of love between how *I* want to be loved and how *you* want to be loved. According to Fromm (1957/1966), "Love is the active concern for the life and the growth of that which we love" (p. 25). He writes that certain basic elements–care, responsibility, respect, and knowledge–are common to all forms of love. Some of the most tragic misalignments of loving can occur when self-knowledge is assumed to be knowledge about the other.

As one woman said to me, "He keeps telling me he loves me, he tells everybody else he loves me, and as he loves me in his way I feel like a pate de foie gras goose that is being stuffed with food I hate. My eyes are burning, my throat is sore, I yearn for different food, the kind I've asked for. But as I'm being lovingly force-fed on someone else's definition of love, I am torn between guilt that I somehow cannot experience this as love, and deep resentment that my individual unique desires for the kind of love I would appreciate are so totally ignored while the indulgent display continues. Sometimes he blames me and says that I am never satisfied. Indeed, this is true–I can never be satisfied when I am blamed for not liking that for which I never expressed a preference, and ultimately have come to loathe. The alternative is a desensitization of my own desires, my unique needs, and a fundamental alienation from my organismic self."

It seems a simple matter if you love someone, to love them in the way they want to be loved. However, this has rarely been any child's experience. Too often we were loved in a way that suited our parents. Jamel had to put on a sweater when his mother was cold, Lila said that her mother wore her like an expensive brooch as public testimony to what a good mother she was. Indeed, loving someone in the way that he or she wants to be loved calls for considerable consciousness and a commitment to the relationship, instead of just using your partner as a vicarious receptacle for your own unmet needs. If she takes a longer time and needs soft music and sweet words to become sexually aroused, it seems a matter of both selfish and loving interest to do this. Perhaps he likes to be jumped on the stairs or groped in the restaurant in order to feel turned on, so perhaps what is needed is that she does that for him. Any couple or couples therapist can probably adduce many more examples of similar negotiable or change-able behaviors, communication patterns, or present-giving styles.

Contracts for change behavior are often quite easy to implement providing there is rational goodwill between the couple and they are willing to acknowledge each other as different (not worse). This can, of course, only happen when there is care, responsibility, and respect for the other person. One of the most important things to realize is that it is not the objective reality of, for example, whether or not there is a draught, that settles disputes between couples and avoids war, but an understanding of each other's subjective experiences–each one's inner phenomenological world. Changes to one's holistical perception can be experienced as extremely threatening.

Because I have always been interested in the bringing down of walls and the building of bridges of understanding, I booked the first possible flight to Berlin on 11th November 1989 on hearing that the Wall was being demolished. One of the most enlightening insights gained from this experience was the incredible psychological threat which people experienced in very suddenly changing their frame of reference. Festinger (1957) referred to this as "cognitive dissonance." Whereas many people welcomed and celebrated the change, for some border guards the challenge was too much.

> No precise figures are yet available but when the Berlin Wall fell, several East German soldiers chose to commit suicide. Rather than attempt to make the painful transition to a new reality where those who yesterday were the "enemy" today become the "friend," some guards preferred the strange safety of death. (Clarkson in George, 1990, p. 14)

Of course the problems of peace in Germany have by no means solved the excruciating problems still facing the country in the future. A decision to stay in the marriage or to try again, does not necessarily mean that the work is ended–sometimes the hardest work has still to follow the reconciliation.

Somewhere I have learned the phrase that "feelings are facts." In working with couples and organizations this is certainly true. Another saying is "A man convinced against his will, is of the same opinion still." The husband experiences his wife as shouting at him when she raises her voice. She doesn't define it as shouting but his feeling constitutes a *fact* in the couple's domain, whether or not it can be shown to be consistent with objective decibel measurements. If she genuinely wants to solve the problem she could find a way of assessing, or responding to a signal from him, when her voice grows so loud that he can no longer pay attention to the content of what she is trying to say to him.

> Morocco and Algeria quarrel over a section of the Western Sahara; . . . The detailed history and geography of the Western Sahara, no matter how carefully studied and documented, is not the stuff with which one puts to rest that kind of territorial dispute. As useful as looking for objective reality can be, it is

ultimately the reality as each side sees it that constitutes the problem in a negotiation and opens the way to a solution. (Fisher & Ury, 1981/1983, pp. 22-23)

Unchangeable Aspects

This is the category which concerns those aspects of the self which are essentially unchangeable, or very hard to change without injury to one's integrity in some important way. In this case the issues are not about attitudes or behavior; they have to do with selfhood. It concerns those deepest characteristics of what we feel as our integrity, authenticity, or those values which are not open to change. This category includes the kinds of values, beliefs or convictions for which people may choose to be martyred rather than change. It is very important to note that these are not demands on the other person to be different (as in the unacceptable category), but are essential qualities or convictions of the self. "This is who I am. This is who you are."

The reasons that couples or nations give for making war, coming together or seceding are varied and complex. The act of seceding is here defined (MacDonald, 1972) as: "to withdraw, esp. from a party, religious body, federation, or the like" (p. 1329). I use this phrase because it covers national choices to declare independence, as well as implying separation or divorce on the smaller scale of the human couple. Rarely are the reasons stated in the official communiques the same as those experienced by the ordinary soldiers or the people of a country. The separating effect when difference exceeds the interest in keeping connected is exemplified in the process of states seceding from the Soviet Union.

On a recent visit to Russia to teach Gestalt (which coincided with the Second Russian Revolution), we met Russians of all political, national and religious persuasions. As we talked with people it became clear that sometimes the urge for individuality becomes stronger than the desire for commonality or bonding. This also happens in couples relationships, sometimes as a result of one or both partners changing as a result of therapy, personal counselling or another impetus to personal growth and change.

Heraclitus said (Guerriere, 1980) that war is "the father of all things" (p. 91). From a Gestalt perspective, healthy aggression is the root of all good human contact and the ground for intimacy. It is our need for others and for intimate intercourse which is one of the most fundamental of human needs (Fairbairn, 1952). The root of the word aggression is "to reach out" (Clarkson, 1989, p. 10). I believe that because we, as human beings, have not yet learnt how to be comfortable with and constructively channel our aggressiveness, we still have such enormous potential for imminent destruction. Although the threat of nuclear war seems to be receding, there is still the possibility that we may die engorged with the detritus of our unthinking, uncaringly aggressive exploitation of our planet. Whether it is the war between the Serbs and the Croats in Yugoslavia, or *The War of the Roses* on our cinema screens, the eternal tension between Eros and Thanatos, between love and war, continues to preoccupy the individual human soul in the dark and lonely night hours, and spills the blood of children in the streets of Beirut.

I am not saying that these characteristics, beliefs or preferences cannot be influenced, modified, or shaped in important ways. I am emphasizing a category of problem which, in some crucial sense, constitutes concerns about the essence of the personality of one or both of the partners. Such unchangeable areas do not necessarily always remain unchangeable. For example, people may change their religious convictions over time or due to circumstance. However, at the time that the couple comes for help it is often very helpful to separate out the issues which fall into this category. They do not threaten the viability of couples work in the same way as those concerns in the unacceptable behavior category. However, getting caught up in turning a basically shy, introverted person into an extraverted, life-of-the-party soul in order to please a wife who has grown more socially confident over time, may demand a fruitless quest from the couples therapist. A highly-sexed husband with a wife who is naturally not very interested in sex may make some adjustments to each other, but sometimes their temperamental preferences for frequency of lovemaking may never truly be compatible. Each may have to compromise their own natural preferences. Tragically sometimes, even though they love each other, a couple may choose to separate rather than live for all their lives with a partner whose fundamental life-rhythms are completely out of synch. For the purposes of this paper I will highlight three such minimally unchangeable areas: temperament, personality, and sexual arousal or preferences.

Temperament, or what I call one's *first nature*, is one such practically unchangeable area. Sometimes people may even try to change their basic temperamental type, but they cannot do it. More importantly, I think they should not because, if they did, they would be violating some important aspect of their organismic integrity which no human being can do for long without damage to themselves and perhaps others. I have referred to this as first nature to distinguish it from *second nature*. I have been concerned over many years as a psychotherapist with the potential oppressiveness for mental or emotional health, of externally imposed criteria, rather than due respect for the intrinsic temperament of each unique human being.

Studies (for example, Thomas et al., 1977) have shown that babies have identifiably different temperaments (which are genetically transmitted), even at birth. In later life these temperamental traits may remain unchanged or may be somewhat modified by environmental circumstances. Damage may be done to children whose temperamental styles are very different from that of their parents, and the parents may be unwilling to see, respect, and value such temperamental difference (Rowe, 1988). Rowe has also drawn attention to the importance of valuing temperamental differences. Personality typologies, for example that of Jung (1944) which was further developed by Myers-Briggs (1976), have also been very useful in helping to differentiate between very different personality types but removing any implication that some are better or healthier than others.

Eysenck (1968) compiled substantial independent research which indicated that people are different in terms of their neuropsychological make-up, their learning styles, and their personality types. The introvert can probably never change the biochemical-electrical activity of his cortex to resemble that of his extrovert friend. The task for therapists, as well as friends, partners, spouses and parents is to value and celebrate each other's different qualities, rather than to do violence to them according to some standard of mass conformity, quoting what some expert or statistical report defines as *normal* or *healthy*. Temperament is defined (Freedman et al., 1975) as "Inborn, constitutional predisposition to react in a specific way to stimuli" (p. 2607). Personality and character can be changed; temperament can but be allowed for, influenced and enjoyed.

> Psychotherapists can avoid getting involved with a fruitless quest for this type of change by (amongst other procedures) clarifying contracts, checking third-party involvement, learning about the physiological bases of behaviour and forever being vigilant against the cardinal sin of the amateur psychologist–extrapolating from your own psychology. Script is not changing *who* we are, but *how* we are in the most important aspects of our lives. (Clarkson, 1988, pp. 22-32)

Another type of unchangeable area is that of one's deepest convictions, such as religious beliefs or political views. A woman who is an Orthodox Jewess is deeply in love with a man who returns her love. He is not Jewish and does not want to convert. He will not and cannot consider in his integrity that, should they marry, their children would be brought up in the Jewish faith. One's heart goes out to such potential couples, thwarted by differences of religion, politics, divisions of war, opposing families, such as played out in the tragedies of Romeo and Juliet, or Heloise and Abelard. Perhaps in our more modern world such loves do not have to end in suicide or convents. However, the unfulfilled yearning for a soulmate which has been found, yet cannot be celebrated, must constitute one of the deepest and most abiding injustices of human destiny.

Of almost similar poignancy are differences which concern the most fundamental biologically-based responses, for example, sexual arousal. In a couple where the man needs to cross-dress in order to become sexually aroused and his wife responds to this with physiological feelings of disgust or revulsion, the couples therapist may be faced with a long-standing and difficult issue which may indeed end in war, if not secession. If she can overcome her physiological responses enough to trade some of her fantasies with some of his, there may be a very satisfactory conclusion. However, wherever this is not possible, the love which brought them together may ultimately be shot through with the bitter ashes of resentful self-sacrifice or the incessant gnawing of guilt, knowing that we are asking someone else to do something which they, at a physiological level, find deeply offensive. I often refer to the *animal* in each of us–the layer of chemical attraction or repulsion which may have to do with the rhinencephalon–one of the oldest structures in the brain associated with smell and therefore with pheromones. How our partners smell to us is an ineradicable element of sexual arousal.

These are the differences that lead to war–when Islam is pitted against Christianity, or northern and southern Irish kill each other in terrorist attacks. Difference of personality, conviction, or physiology is probably the source of the greatest tragedy of human existence as well as the fount of the greatest joy. Because it is in these differences between individuals, partners, nations, that diversity can flourish and variety can come to flower. When there is an erosion of such differences there is a drift towards conformity, an imposition of the norm of mediocrity, and an attenuation of sexual desire in the couple.

Perhaps we can change our attitudes towards such differences, and the couples therapist can help the couple towards working on accepting and celebrating such differences. Of course, frequently the qualities that first attracted us to a partner can become the source of later irritation. An ambitious high-powered woman executive who married a gentle, sensitive residential social worker who has no ambition except to become more perfectly attuned with nature, needs to decide before she marries him that this is who he is and make a commitment that she will not embark on a change program to turn him into somebody different later in the relationship. The same may apply to him. If she needs to be active, energetic, and goal-achieving, and this is healthy and good for her, it is very necessary that he be willing to support her in her self-actualization, however different it may be from his. If they can do this, this mutual appreciation of each other's different qualities, can become and remain the core of a continuing spring of wonderment, pleasure, and creative tension, mutually enhancing each other's lives from different sources. All of us have the drawbacks of our virtues and for the long-term loving couple it is essential to separate out changes in attitudes and behavior, which may be necessary or desirable, from changes in the essential quality of the person which, in effect, would make them very different from the person you love.

CONCLUSION

In this paper I have briefly surveyed three major categories of conflict and negotiation between couples and I have also briefly juxtaposed these with similar issues between nations at war, at peace, and in the process of secession. I hope that I have shown the importance of separating issues to do with human rights from issues between equal negotiating partners, and that I have made the beginnings of the case for the importance of celebrating difference, modifying the drawbacks of our virtues, but cherishing the qualities in our partners which, by their very otherness, become the fulcrum for greatest attraction and most significant mutual transformation. Although I cannot in any ultimately significant way influence the fates of nations, I hope that this perspective on how to effect the fate of loving, warring, or separating couples may prove useful to others who are also engaged in the endeavor to be a better, loving partner and the struggle to make this a better world.

REFERENCES

Bach, G., and Goldberg, H. (1983). *Creative aggression: The art of assertive living*. London: Anchor Books. (Original work published 1974)

Berne, E. (1980). *Transactional analysis in psychotherapy*. London: Souvenir Press. (First published 1961)

Caplan, P. J. (1985). *The myth of women's masochism*. New York: E. P. Dutton.

Clarkson, P. (1988). Script cure?–a diagnostic pentagon of types of therapeutic change, *Transactional Analysis Journal, 18*(30), 211-219.

Clarkson, P. (1989). *Gestalt counselling in action*. London: Sage.

Clarkson, P. (1990). Despair before change, *Counselling News, 1*, 11.

Clarkson, P. (1991). Facets of the dance, *Journal of Couples Therapy, 2*(3), 71-82.

Dorfman, A. (1992). *Death and the maiden*. London: Nick Hern Books. (First published 1991)

Dryden, W. (Ed.) (1985). *Marital therapy in Britain* (Vols 1 and 2). London: Harper & Row.

Eysenck, H. J. (1968). *Handbook of abnormal psychology*. London: Pitman. Medical Publishing Co. Ltd.

Fairbairn, W. R. D. (1952). *Psycho-analytic studies of the personality*. London: Tavistock.

Festinger, L. (1957). *A theory of cognitive dissonance*. Stanford: Stanford University Press.

Fisher, R., and Ury, W. (1983). *Getting to yes*. London: Hutchinson.

Freedman, A. M., Kaplan, H. I., and Sadock, B. J. (1975). *Comprehensive textbook of psychiatry–II*. Baltimore: The Williams and Wilkins Company.

Fromm, E. (1966). *The art of loving*. London: Unwin Books. (Original work published 1957)

Gellert, S. D. (1983). *Nuts come in pairs*. Huntington Station, NY: Cite Press Inc.

George, E. (1990). Shortwave: Heard in the global village (interview with P. Clarkson) *Wave*, (Autumn 1990), 14.

Guerriere, D. (1980). Physis, Sophia, Psyche, in J. Sallis and K. Maly (Eds.), *Heraclitean fragments: A companion volume to the Heidegger/Fink seminar on Heraclitus* (pp. 87-134). Alabama: University of Alabama Press.

Jung, C. G. (1944). *Psychological types or the psychology of individuation*. (H. G. Baynes, Trans.). London: Kegan Paul, Trench, Trubner.

MacDonald, A. M. (1972). *Chambers twentieth century dictionary*. Edinburgh: T. & A. Constable. (First published 1901)

Makhoere, C. K. (1988). *No child's play*. London: The Women's Press Ltd.

Miller, A. (1985). *That shalt not be aware: Society's betrayal of the child*. (H. and H. Hannum, Trans.). London: Pluto Books. (Original work published 1981)

Miller, A. (1987). *The drama of being a child*. (R. Ward, Trans.). London: Virago. (Original work published 1979)

Myers, K. C., and Briggs Myers, I. (1976). *Myers-Briggs type indicator*. Palo Alto, California: Consulting Psychologists Press.

Rowe, D. (1988). *The successful self*. London: Fontana/Collins.

Satir, V. (1978). *Conjoint family therapy*. London: Souvenir Press. (First published 1967)

Thomas, A. L., Chess, S., and Birch, H. (1977). *Temperament and development*. New York: Brunner/Mazel.

"Talk to Me Like
I'm Someone You Love—"
Conflict Intervention for Real Life

Nancy Dreyfus

SUMMARY. A method of changing set for combative couples was presented in which written messages are used to refocus combatants from their specific controversy to how they are relating to each other. We see how these so-called *Flash Cards* move a couple from content to process, providing a face-saving medium for the validation of feelings and the expression of caring. It is theorized that the most transformative aspect of the intervention is the ability to provide alienated partners with a much-needed template of giving and receiving, "reminding them" of what a positive bond is supposed to feel like.

Imagine, Reader, that you and your partner are having a tense, pretty unpleasant evening with each other, veering back and forth between hostility and restraint.

You both seemed in good moods earlier at home, happily anticipating dinner out together at a new restaurant. But something started to shift, it seems, when a little piece of behavior on the part of one of you was experienced by the other as "significant."

Perhaps the one of you who worries more about being late, developed the notion that the more casual one was being passive-aggressive when he or she became engrossed in a piece of junk

Nancy Dreyfus has a PsyD from Hahnemann University in Philadelphia and a Masters from the Columbia School of Journalism. She is involved in supervising psychotherapists who wish to integrate their formal training with their spiritual reality. She is in private practice at 1002 Severn Ln., Wynnewood, PA 19096.

95

mail, when it was obviously time to be picking up the baby-sitter. Or, maybe one of you feels convinced that the other's witty comment on how you handled your most difficult borderline that morning, was critical and undermining and shows that he or she has completely missed the wisdom behind your whole approach with this client. Maybe one of you started to put on an item of clothing that you "know" the other one detests.

Whatever the scenario–and feel free to make up your own–it's not particularly friendly getting into the car, even though apologies have been made and there's a renewed commitment "to have a good time." Something has just gotten out of kilter in a familiar way between you, and it continues to be one of those evenings where you sort of pick at each other, hypersensitive to each other's every word, look and, in particular, intonation.

The thought of trying harder to communicate maturely sounds like the correct thing to do (particularly since one or both of you happen to be psychotherapists who pride yourselves on excellent listening and reflective skills–not to mention your true love for each other). But this thought of shifting gears and attempting to process it all, also gives rise to a tired, anxious feeling. Each of you feels justifiably "right"–about who knows what?–and sees the other as being rigid, if not willful. Both of you feel misperceived and unappreciated. Maybe you're even having thoughts like, "What am I doing with this impossible person?"

Now, imagine that you're back home–irritable, weary and nervous that things could deteriorate a few more notches between you. And now, imagine that this impossible person leaves you for a moment, comes back with a little card in hand, looks you kindly in the eye, and holds up this message for you to read:

"I LOVE YOU, I HATE FIGHTING AND CAN WE PLEASE HUG?"

How would you feel?

Now, it is you who is willing to move beyond the unpleasantness and make an offering of goodwill to your partner. What would you imagine the result would be if you handed him or her this communiqué:

"WHAT CAN I SAY THAT WOULD MAKE YOU FEEL UNDERSTOOD?" Or this one:

"YOU DIDN'T DO ANYTHING WRONG.
IT'S MY OWN CRAZINESS–
TRUST ME TO GET THROUGH IT."

Finally, think of times throughout your history with this partner or any other, of how refreshing, if not useful, it might have been to present this person with some of the following messages–or, on the other hand, to have been the recipient of them:

"IF YOU COULD TELL ME
THAT YOU LOVE ME AND
CARE ABOUT ME, IT WOULD
BE A LOT EASIER TO HEAR
YOUR CRITICISM."

"TALK TO ME LIKE
I'M SOMEONE
YOU LOVE."

"I'M FEELING DEFENSIVE.
CAN YOU SAY THIS IN A
GENTLER WAY SO I CAN
FEEL SAFE WITH YOU?"

"I REALIZE I WAS MAKING
A BIG DEAL OUT OF
SOMETHING THAT'S
JUST NOT THAT
IMPORTANT. I'VE LET IT
GO."

"I DON'T LIKE HOW THIS IS
GOING. LET'S START AGAIN
AND *REALLY* LISTEN TO
EACH OTHER."

"WHEN YOU DON'T
RESPOND TO ME, I
I FEEL ABANDONED."

"I'M SCREAMING SO LOUD
BECAUSE I FEEL SO
HUMILIATED."

"I'VE SAID SOME MEAN
THINGS. CAN I TAKE
THEM BACK?"

These are a few examples of what I've come to call *Flash Cards for Real Life*™ (see also Figure 1), a conflict intervention tool that I have been developing with couples in my practice, colleagues and friends, and using personally with my husband, a psychiatrist. As of this writing my husband's preferred *Flash Card* is, "RIGHT NOW I DON'T NEED A THERAPIST. I NEED YOUR LOVE."

I like to think of the cards as a "realness-accessing" tool that, hopefully, will move an angry or out-of-contact couple towards a

FIGURE 1. Flash Cards for Real Life™

Talk to me like I'm someone you love.

I'm feeling defensive.
Can you say this in a gentler way,
so that I can feel safe with you?

I guess I haven't been listening very well.
Please give me another chance.

What can I say
that would make you feel understood?

I know I sound like a maniac,
but I haven't stopped loving you.

I'm sorry.

When you talk to me in that tone of voice,
I feel humiliated.

Please stop yelling. You're scaring me.

I don't like how this is going.
Let's start again and *really* listen to each other.

When you don't respond to me,
I feel abandoned.

saner way of being with each other. I continue to be struck by the healing effect on intimate combatants when a little decency is thrown in the face of their usual patterns of defensiveness, irritability, withdrawal and terrible listening.

When *Flash Cards* work, which is frequently the case, the sense of upset that two frustrated–even furious–people are feeling can melt almost instantly into increased civility and a sense of relief. When couples experience the messages as heartfelt, a kind of safety gets established where it is not unusual for real feelings of love, playfulness and appreciation to be evoked in the midst of what minutes earlier looked like thick, mutual hostility.

I dreamed up the cards during one tense couples session with a brainy, critical and narcissistically vulnerable social services administrator and her counterpart husband, an engineering professor. Jenna and Carl are a good example of the angry, articulate, fairly psychologically aware woman who overwhelms her slower-thinking partner with her emotions, perceptions and constant analysis.

As Jenna was getting more cutting and out of control on the topic of Carl's "embarrassingly low level responses to movies," Carl became increasingly vague, defensive and then silently exasperated. Carl perceived his wife as unfair, unreachable and unstoppable–in short, he saw her as crazed enough to be ignored. Made more anxious and infuriated by her husband's unresponsiveness, Jenna restated her criticisms, only more harshly.

Impulsively, I grabbed a piece of paper lying around and wrote a message for Carl to hold up to Jenna: "TALK TO ME LIKE I'M SOMEONE YOU LOVE."

In just a moment Jenna calmed herself down and seemed to be, in one blow, a bit disoriented, humbled and sweetened. She re-oriented herself to soften her communication to her husband in a way I had never observed before in my office.

Carl took immediate pleasure in this turn of events. ("She must love me if she's willing to make such a nice change–and so fast.") His subsequent movement, in fact, from "turned-off" to nicely engaged, was probably more dramatic than Jenna's toning down. Having had the experience of reaching his wife, he was now willing to respond to her disappointment in a more responsible and gratifying manner.

From that session on, flash card production fell under the rubric of the *"Talk to me like I'm someone you love"* ™ project. Together, Jenna, Carl and I created a number of additional cards for them including: "I KNOW I SOUND LIKE A MANIAC, BUT I HAVEN'T STOPPED LOVING YOU," and "WHEN YOU GO ON AND ON LIKE THAT, I GET AFRAID YOU WON'T STOP."

At present I've designed and printed 70 generic *Flash Cards for Real Life*™ and attached the set at one corner with a basic looseleaf ring. The messages are indexed sequentially; attempts to index them thematically for speedier, more spontaneous crisis intervention proved tedious and so highly subjective, that I suspect the task is impossible.

Flash Cards comes with an additional number of blank bordered cards for couples to create their own personalized messages. These might be premeditated ones to have on hand ("I AM NOT YOUR FATHER. I AM MARTY WHO LOVES YOU AND WANTS YOU TO BE HAPPY") or messages concocted in the tenseness, meanness or paralysis of the moment in order to re-establish contact and goodwill ("I'M SORRY I ATTACKED YOU. I REALLY WANTED YOU TO KNOW HOW IGNORED I FELT AT THE PARTY–AND I KNOW I WENT OVERBOARD").

Whether couples use the printed cards or simply write messages to each other on torn envelopes, there is something about the way the printed word can dramatically "change the energy" that merits attention as a clinical tool in our efforts to teach clients what a powerful dissolver of distance, their willingness to be genuine can be. To find out that being genuine "works," that one's own realness is inherently friendly, connective and peace-producing (and not alienating, as often feared) is a cornerstone of good couples work.

The word "realness" here, definitely includes the making of "I statements." But thinking too, of the kind of effect we might want a written message to have on two contentious people, being real also means making any statement where one partner acknowledges, directly or by the structure of his language, that *how* the two of them are relating to the issue *is* the issue. In other words, the *Flash Card* refocuses our contentious duo on how they're relating to each other.

This is one of the reasons why, I think, the basic "Talk to me like

I'm someone you love" *Flash Card* itself, is often such an appealing and powerful intervention.

Since so much of intimate combat has to do with the re-creation of childhood hurts, mostly having to do with the self not feeling loved, respected or validated, (Hendrix, 1988; Pierrakos, 1990) a simple, but firm request to be treated in a loving manner, can immediately put us in touch with our dignity, make us remember who we are and how we deserve to be treated–and importantly, invite our partner to treat us as we are now treating ourselves. Even expressed as a demand, it is a demand freed of any harshness because of the integrity it presupposes.

Though we usually don't think about our childhoods in this way, most of us grew up with parents who loved us–*but who didn't characteristically talk to us like they did*. If, by some miracle, as children we had been in touch enough with ourselves to confront a difficult parent with the affirmation, "Talk to me like I'm someone you love!" we would have at once been in touch with our pain, with our self worth . . . and with our parent. From this point-of-view, the phrase is a deeply empowering and relational one. I would add here that any *Flash Card* transaction carries the potential meta-message, "Let's talk to each other like we love each other."

Obviously, one doesn't need a *Flash Card* to communicate this phrase, or any other. But try, in the midst of hostilities, to verbalize "Talk to me like I'm someone you love!" without counter-productive annoyance, insistence, or, at best, self-righteousness. Somehow, by going straight to the heart, the printed word also goes to the heart of the matter.

Like many of our clients, much of our own personal growth has to do with an interpersonal orientation towards life, love and relationships that involves a fair amount of "conscious relating."

This includes a number of precepts which, with the additional impetus of the recovery/co-dependency/wounded child movement (Beattie, 1987; Whitfield, 1987; Woititz, 1985), are now becoming part of general contemporary wisdom:

- Love yourself as a prerequisite for loving anyone else.
- Be in touch with your feelings and be comfortable sharing them–assertively, when necessary.

- Be vulnerable, yet set good boundaries with others.
- Withhold judgements and don't take things personally.
- Make "I" statements and avoid blaming.
- Convey unconditional support of your partner's beingness, even when you can't stand what he's doing.
- Practice forgiveness of oneself and others.
- *Really* listen.

As a psychotherapist, wife and observer of the day-to-day inter-actions of many presumably "conscious" couples, I am certain that most of us are doing better with the theory part of conscious relating than the practicum. I know how challenging it can be for me at times to stay centered in my goodwill and truth when interactions with people who matter to me start feeling strained, threatening or just familiarly crummy. Any of us can have difficulty getting back on track when a loved one annoys us or when we know we have been the annoying or unkind one and can't quite get to "I'm sorry."

As time goes on without reconciliation, we know the ease with which little upsets can turn into deeper resentments. This is because now, we are also reacting to what looks like our partners' perverse inability to adequately receive our upset and to appreciate what it means to us. In our internal experience, our partners move increas-ingly into the position of "parental imagos" (Hendrix), so that no matter what our initial grievance once was, it now gets overshad-owed by the ancient life-and-death struggle to be heard and taken seriously. From this point-of-view, reconciliation is often a matter of letting go of pride rather than grievances, and it is here that the written word is so useful as a peace offering.

For a couple that has been arguing, the act of refraining from the next uncharitable remark is in itself no small thing. To then go through the effort of finding and offering an appropriate *Flash Card* is often experienced by both parties as a true relational act . . . and a very tender moment. In an instant, the sender has signaled to the receiver:

- that he has given up some of his defenses, not the least of which is pride.
- that he is now making the relationship matter more than his position.

- that he doesn't enjoy holding on to his negativity as much as his partner feared that he did.
- that he really wishes to be closer.
- that magically, he has become a more giving person than he was a few minutes ago. The *Flash Card*, after all, is a gift.

When a couple is in a reactive mode, verbal statements that could potentially move the two in a more peaceful direction sometimes get drowned out in the face of the wounded person's need to hang on to the affront he or she feels to his dignity. Often combatants are too busy thinking up their next remark or, for that matter, strategic action, to hear a conciliatory gesture. Or, if they do hear it, it is not uncommon to focus on some piece of the gesture that could possibly lack conviction, leading the offended party to discount the peace-maker and take further offense at the latter's "insincerity." "Don't think you can shut me up so easily!" is the battle cry of our insincerity-detector.

This is where written messages seem to have an edge. The novelty of the visual format gives them a better than average chance of being received and appreciated. Knowing this gives the sender the courage to make the first move, overcoming the resistance to being the one to "give in." Likewise, the written form neutralizes a certain level of worry about being heard and about being taken seriously.

One doesn't have to be that psychologically aware to appreciate that the offering of a *Flash Card* also implies some emotional risk, and with that awareness, even the most generic of messages (i.e., "I'M SORRY.") seem to be experienced by recipients as sincere and personal.

Though I have conducted no rigorous studies on the issue of written versus oral messages, a number of individuals have mentioned to me in passing that they tried verbalizing *Flash Card* messages that previously, in written form, had had a positive effect on a difficult interaction with the same partner. Not surprisingly, the general feeling seems to be that sharing authentically has some minimum healing effect in any modality; certainly, my hope would be that one result of using *Flash Cards* would be increased naturalness with verbal intimacy.

However, my clients and those of colleagues who have experimented with written messages, report almost universally that the written message is notably more impactful than the spoken one, once the sparring couple has reached the level of conflict where they see each other as adversaries. In Creighton's schema of conflict escalation (1990), this is when an argument becomes a "fight," and the goal of the interaction shifts from resolving an issue to inflicting injury. At this point each party is oriented towards justifying his position and making the other person wrong or bad. This is the time, Creighton writes, when "neither of us is willing to share information about our vulnerabilities" (p. 28). And, I would add, we are even less interested in taking in information about our partner's vulnerabilities.

It is at this point that written messages can give stuck partners an opportunity to change set. The set in need of change is the one generally labeled "needing to be right." Content-wise, there are a number of variations on this basic theme: needing to be right about my innocence, about your culpability, about my reasonableness, about your insensitivity . . . , etc. But if one is willing to give up any illusions about the specialness of his particular bickering, one gets to see that the variations are all but inconsequential. I would add, by the way, that this is probably true for all disputants, whether intimate or international.

The opportunity *Flash Cards* provide is *to choose being loving and contactful over being right.* And to this end, the cards *per se* generally don't let users down; the trick, however, is to make the heroic choice to use them.

I started out using the cards as a pragmatic tool to transmute unproductive communication and to bring couples more into reality with each other. It was only later that I began to appreciate that the very act of one person offering the other a *Flash Card* when the two of them were in an unpleasant, if not miserable space, was providing a teaching tool of another order. At a spiritual level, the lesson the cards provide is that love is a choice, that it is a deliberate, and I would add, moral action that is not inherently predicated on a "warm feeling." It is the choice to honor connection when you're not feeling close and, if you're lucky, inspire a dropping of defenses in your partner.

Rick and Lisa, a young, college-educated couple, both from blue-collar backgrounds, were in my office having a new round in their long-standing battle over Rick's involvement with his parents and brain-damaged older brother. Lisa, who happened to be pregnant, was in a highly charged state, frantic that Rick would "never" be able to choose her and the baby over his parents and brother. Rick felt his wife was being selfish as well as insensitive to the special needs of his family of origin. He was also insulted by her lack of trust in his ability to know his priorities. The two were highly polarized, questioning the marriage and each seeing the other as grossly self-centered. Needless to say, they were not liking each other much.

I pulled out the *Flash Card* "WHAT CAN I SAY THAT WOULD MAKE YOU FEEL UNDERSTOOD?", put it face-down on a table and asked for "a brave volunteer." Rick took the card, studied it, and made a face at me of only partially mock skepticism. I asked him to spend a few moments thinking about the implications of offering the card to his wife and decide whether offering it or not would most honor himself at this point. I told him that under the circumstances, either decision was brave, and I meant it. He waited a minute and held up the card to his wife.

Moved by both the message and her husband's most moderate willingness, Lisa moved out of her attacking mode, curled up and burst into quiet sobs that might be loosely translated as saying, "At last . . . help is on the way . . . someone finally knows what my screaming has been about." She haltingly told her husband that just the fact he wanted her to feel understood made her feel good and right now she didn't need to hear anything more from him. (This reaction, by the way, is extremely common with this card, particularly when the arguing has been protracted and it is offered spontaneously at home, independent of therapeutic suggestion.)

Rick got to see the remarkable possibility that his wife really wanted her fears to be acknowledged more than she wanted to yank him from his family. (Just as importantly, Lisa got to see that too.) He also got to see that he could perform a loving action, offer a real kindness as it were, when he wasn't feeling particularly loving. In my office, in fact, when I asked for a volunteer, he was feeling bitter and vengeful.

Like many clients who have been locked in a tense marital situation, Rick was relieved to experience: that simple, non-dramatic expression of one person's humanity can set two people in a healing direction; that even in our most antagonistic moments we are not that far from our desire and ability to feel a happier connection. His later analysis of using the *Flash Card* expresses a common sentiment: "It was a face-saving way of getting where we both wanted to be in the first place."

If I have given the impression that *Flash Cards* do magic it is only because when they do work it can feel that way. It takes a fair amount of commitment and occasionally, desperation, for a couple to use them independently of the treatment situation–and even here, just as often as a frustrated "last resort" than as some thoughtful, spiritual act. On the other hand, while it is true that not every *Flash Card* transaction results in profound mutual healing, it is also true that it is rare for the cards to be used with no result at all. Somebody will learn something.

A client of mine, a woman of a generally feisty and opinionated nature, reported writing her husband the following message after days of mutual sniping around the issue of the latter's explosiveness with their teenage son: "I CAN SEE THAT WHAT I'M DOING TO YOU IS WORSE THAN WHAT YOU DO TO MATTHEW. I'M SORRY. PLEASE FORGIVE ME." The husband responded sarcastically and remained unmoved.

Though the wife felt at a loss because the message did not seem to touch her husband, she was able to come to the understanding that if this surrender on her part wasn't meaningful to her husband, it was pointless to continue any discussion. She reasoned that anyone in his right mind would accept a sincere apology and she wasn't going to argue with someone who wasn't in his right mind. This bit of reality about his current availability catapulted *her* into her right mind; uncharacteristically, she backed off from both interacting with her husband and her tendency "to relate" regardless of circumstances. She taped her message and dangled it from a kitchen fixture and went about her business.

Two days later, when the husband finally approached her in a relatively rational manner, it was also uncharacteristic for him to take such initiative. In this case, I think, the written message provided the woman with a therapeutic medium around which to integrate a stronger sense of self. She was making a case, more to herself than anyone, for her own goodness and got much value in practicing self-containment. It was this new ability, and not her written message alone, that made an impression on her husband.

It is my usual practice to have a few trial runs with *Flash Cards* in my office before giving a couple a set to take home. Whether clients initially perceive the cards as "dopey," "gimmicky," "fantastic," or "just what we need," there is often some initial self-consciousness in using a communication tool which feels contrived. Reactions along this line are validated and, where appropriate, reframed as part of the couples' pre-existing discomfort with letting go of defensiveness. The idea I want to convey here is that any conciliatory gesture can be thwarted by anticipated awkwardness and that in the spirit of *Flash Cards* themselves, the willingness to do something contrived is in itself a loving thing.

Few clients require more theoretical explanation, but for those who do, I make a point that is expressed beautifully in a spiritually-oriented parenting book by Rolfe (1985), about how a child hears his parent's most abstract message first and the most precise message last. This means that when a furious parent complains about the toys not being picked up, the messages that hit the child the hardest (and therefore preoccupy him) are "Mommy is mad at me," or "Mommy doesn't love me now," or "I disappoint people," or, at worst, "I'm bad." Only after these more abstract and compelling concerns get resolved is the child able to genuinely take in anything useful the mother might have to say about neatness–let alone cheerfully put the toys away.

I give enough explanation of transference, projection and the re-creation of childhood hurts, to make the case for the same principle being at work in most important adult relationships: We hear the most abstract messages first because we tend to be sensitized to them. *Flash Cards* work because they address the interpersonal concerns that underly the most ostensibly mundane interactions. They make use of our natural tendency to listen for and listen to these so-called "abstract" messages.

When clients or, for that matter, colleagues question my belief that a substantial psychic and visceral shift from unfriendly to friendly can be brought about quickly in warring couples, I ask them to consider this common occurrence.

You're driving on the highway and someone thoughtlessly pulls ahead and cuts you off. You feel furious, unnerved, and convinced the other driver is a madman. Then, unbelievably, this "madman" turns around, notices what he's done, shakes his head and slaps his hand to his cheek in a gesture indicating, "What an idiot I've been," and mouths through his car window, "I'm sorry." What happens? Not only does your rage and, perhaps, your judgement diminish radically, but you may even start feeling some vague sense of camaraderie with the fellow. If you don't share a knowing smile, then, at least, the two of you share a brief moment of humanness. Particularly relevant to the theory behind *Flash Cards*, the other driver no longer seems like a dangerous person to you.

How did this transformation take place . . . and so quickly?

Consider the possibility that the root of interpersonal upset in this incident has more to do with the hurt, fear and even humiliation that come from feeling unacknowledged and uncared for–and by a total stranger who almost just killed you!–than it does from the fact that you were in physical danger. If there was little of an interpersonal nature in this situation, our survival alone would relieve much of our emotional discomfort, but, in fact, it does not. A situation with a similar emotional tone can occur when a spouse is two hours late for dinner with no phone call and we're feeling truly worried as to his or her whereabouts. His return will eliminate our worry about his safety, but not the feelings associated with his perceived failure to think about our worry–particularly if he seems bent on justifying his lateness.

Whether we are the aforementioned driver, the worried or the "thoughtless" spouse, or the couple going out to dinner at the beginning of this article, we will move out of our angry posture only when some safety has been introduced into a situation that feels emotionally threatening. I believe that safety gets reinstated in a polarized couple when there is a shared recognition that a non-judgmental, unifying connection exists between them and that this connection *matters*. Prather and Prather (1988), who have exquisitely analyzed the subtle and usually unconscious ways couples prevent themselves from their desire to unite, go so far as to state that until the intention to join with each other is made explicit by the couple, conflict remains unresolved.

So even with our drivers, it's not the apology *per se* that heals negative emotions. If instead of saying, "I'm sorry," the offending driver had said, "Don't hate me," or "I must have scared you," or "My wife just bawled me out," a similar result could have been produced. Or, even if you, the victim has said in a matter-of-fact way to the guy, "You know, that was pretty dangerous," this too, could have created a neutral, if not friendly, outcome. Why? Because the very sending of the message is a relational act honoring some human connection between you. And because the content of the message is so real.

Since I think there is a basic common sense about why the offering of written messages would be healing, further philosophizing on the topic feels a little like giving more explanation as to why telling a loved one "I love you" is a good idea. We have already seen how written messages move a couple from content to process, can provide immediate acknowledgement of both parties' feelings and show tangible evidence of caring. They are also an explicit statement from one partner to the other of his or her willingness to be joined, or, at least to move towards joining.

Yet, the swiftness with which I have seen truly militant couples melt with the presentation of relatively unremarkable written notes ("I GUESS I HAVEN'T BEEN LISTENING VERY WELL. PLEASE GIVE ME ANOTHER CHANCE.") has challenged me to further expand my thinking about the theoretical basis of *Flash Cards*.

This is my thought:

When couples are feeling victimized and defensive, locked into what Lerner (1985) calls "the dance of anger," the emotional relevance and resonance of any particular *Flash Card* message is helpful and often calming, but not necessarily transformative. What I've come to see as transformative is the introduction into the combat zone of a transaction that basically consists of two vital ingredients: giving and receiving. Corny as it may sound, these are the building blocks of love and I believe that the transaction reminds combatants of what they are fighting to regain in the first place.

The simple giving of something and the receiving of it–and with all respect for my language skills, a plain white rag might be quite effective—is a rehearsal for sanity. It makes couples remember that something exists that feels better than fighting, and that they are, indeed, capable of producing that something. When my husband hands me his latest creation, "YOU CALL *THIS* TALKING TO SOMEONE LIKE YOU LOVE THEM? ARE YOU KIDDING?" I am sobered by the message, but more affected by the mini give-and-take between us.

The war is on its way out when we remember that being given to feels good and that perhaps, being received, feels even better.

REFERENCES

Beattie, M. (1987) *Co-dependent no more*. San Francisco: Harper/Hazleden.

Creighton, J. (1990) *Don't go away mad*. New York: Doubleday.

Hendrix, H. (1988) *Getting the love you want: A Guide for Couples*. New York: Holt and Company.

Lerner, H. (1985) *The dance of anger*. New York: Harper & Row.

Pierrakos, E. (1990) The compulsion to recreate and overcome childhood hurts. *The pathwork of self-transformation*. New York: Bantam.

Prather, G. and Prather, H. (1988) *A book for couples*. New York: Bantam.

Rolfe, R. (1985) *You can postpone anything but love*. Edgemont, PA.: Ambassador Press.

Whitfield, C. (1987) *Healing the child within*. Deerfield Beach, FL.: Health Communications.

Woititz, J. (1985) *Struggle for intimacy*. Deerfield Beach, FL.: Health Communications.

The Tasks and Traps of Relationships

Lawrence Maltin
Joan D. Atwood

SUMMARY. This article approaches relationships from primarily a systemic-psychodynamic framework in that psychoanalytic interpretations and assumptions are integrated into a basic systemic orientation. The paper focuses on the prerelationship developmental tasks, relationship developmental tasks, the role of love and intimacy in emotional maturity, and the traps and pitfalls commonly encountered by couples, as illustrated by the activation of protective, defensive mechanisms. The material is illustrated by a case presentation. Implications for counseling are considered throughout.

"This is definitely not the man I married! I can't believe this! I can't reach him. He was never like this." Such exclamations are common in marital counseling offices where combinations of shock, dismay, hurt, frustration, and anger are presented, as couples struggle to understand what happened to that blissful time prior to marriage. They ponder how conditions could have so dramatically

---

Lawrence Maltin, MD, is a psychiatrist and psychoanalyst and is Medical Director of Alternative Recovery Programs, a drug and alcohol rehabilitation facility in Garden City, NY, 11530. He has a private practice in Woodbury and Garden City, NY, and has done extensive work in the area of psychoanalytic psychotherapy. He has also published in the field of psychotherapy.

Joan D. Atwood, PhD, CSW, is Coordinator of the Graduate Programs in Marriage and Family Therapy and the Director of the Marital and Family Clinic at Hofstra University, Hempstead, NY, 11550. She is the author of *Treatment Techniques for Common Mental Disorders* (NY: Aronson, 1987) and *Family Therapy: A Cognitive-Behavioral Approach* (release 2/92), has done extensive research and written numerous journal articles in the field of marriage and family therapy.

Please send all reprint requests to Joan D. Atwood.

111

changed from the time before they were married when they were so in love to the disappointment, hurt, and anger so prevalent in their marriage now. Most couples are hardly prepared for the complexity of processes that are set in motion when the marital contract is sealed. It is most often the first time that the individuals are assuming full responsibility for their own lives, and separating from their primary families of origin to whom strong attachments and dependencies had been formed. The multitude of issues that begin to emerge in the marital union are apt initially to be dispatched with a confident, "We'll work it out. We love each other." In the throes of romantic love and sexual attraction, it is difficult for couples to consider what it is going to be like looking across the breakfast table at their partner day after day. Later, after the negative cycles of interaction are evident and the individuals are worn out from trying to work it out, they present for couple therapy with a sense of failure often stating, "We're unhappy. We can't seem to stop fighting." It is the purpose of this paper to explore the psychological developmental tasks necessary for the formation of a healthy, stable relationship. These tasks are examined premaritally and in a marital situation. Psychological factors hindering the completion of these tasks are presented, along with a discussion of the traps and pitfalls commonly encountered by couples who have not completed the tasks. Implications for couple therapy are considered throughout.

PRERELATIONSHIP DEVELOPMENTAL TASKS

Partners in a healthy marriage are continuously changing and growing with respect to their personality development, interests, goals and relationships with friends, relatives, and colleagues. In order for these changes to benefit the marital relationship, flexibility and sensitivity are required on each person's part. This in turn necessitates the maturational skills necessary to cope with the partner's growth and define it as a benefit rather than as a threat. Marriage often highlights and intensifies the emotional challenges necessary to achieve greater personal maturity, which in turn, contributes to greater marital happiness. Personal maturity involves the successful negotiation of life tasks that each individual must face.

These tasks include: (a) The formation of a positive self-image which fosters spontaneity, curiosity, and more competent intellectual and social skills; (b) The separation and individuation of the person from their parents into a more self-reliant, and confident individual; (c) The development of healthy self-esteem which allows for the expression of capacities to love and give to others without feeling depleted or deprived; (d) The willingness to assume responsibilities and care-taking positions without feeling resentful or taken advantage of; and (e) The capacity to achieve a balance in one's mental functioning between reasoning and emotions which allows one to develop the ability to empathize with another's feelings and position (Mahler, 1975).

An emotionally mature relationship requires mutual respectfulness of each partner's growth and changing needs and interests. More mature individuals can accommodate changing dimensions in their partners without feeling rejected, diminished, or threatened. They feel comfortable pursuing outside interests and bringing other important people into the marital relationship sphere. Although the capacity to function independently in a marriage is most important, the ability to trust and rely on one's partner is an equally vital issue. Meissner (1978) states this clearly when he discusses separation/individuation as discussed by Mahler:

> The successful negotiation of the developmental tasks leads . . . in the direction of a progressively more differentiated and internally integrated organization of the sense of self and the gradual establishment of an identity which reflects the unique psychological organization of that growing individual and which provides the bulwark for the working through and successful resolution of developmental crises and the inevitable complexities and conflicts of human life. (p. 32)

More secure individuals, who have come into the marriage after completing the basic developmental tasks, are able to recognize and share fears, insecurities, and limitations, which allows for a reaching out in times of need, stress, or problems. In this way, both partners feel they are making important contributions to each other, which enhances the feeling of mutual dignity and respectfulness. While this issue of equality and mutual respectfulness may not be emphasized in other cultures, in American society where equality is a significant issue, it is a crucial factor in the smooth functioning of a marriage.

RELATIONSHIP DEVELOPMENTAL TASKS

When one considers the requirements necessary for two married people to remain contented through modern day stresses, obligations, and economic, personal, and social pressures, it is important to give and discuss matters which will deeply affect the individual, the partnership, and the eventual family unit.

A successful marriage involves accomplishing fundamental tasks which we will be discussing throughout this paper. Some of the more basic developmental tasks are: (a) Continuing to grow as separate individuals in the marriage, while maintaining a working interdependence with themselves and society (Erikson, 1968). This growth process is what is involved in one's maturing as a person and being respectful of the partner's individuality. It means working out differences in backgrounds, past experiences, and intellectual and personality styles with a spirit of cooperation rather than a power struggle; (b) Bridging the transition from romantic love to the caring and nurturing involved in a longer term intimate relationship; (c) Learning to compromise one's own needs with the needs of one's partner so that resentments and feelings of deprivations are held to a minimum; (d) Mutual agreement on the division of labor within the household so that the workload of marriage and raising a family is equally shared; (e) The ability to make the transition from the initial romantic dyad or couple to the inclusion of children which brings about important changes in the relationship of the couple; (f) The effective management of conflict which is an inevitable accompaniment of a healthy relationship where both partners are expressive of their thoughts, feelings, and needs; and (g) Maintaining sexual interest so that the marital relationship is the primary relationship in both its emotional and physical aspects. Blanck and Blanck (1968) list a number of ways in which the marital relationship is one of the most significant human experiences which can foster individual development.

THE ROLE OF LOVE AND INTIMACY
IN EMOTIONALLY MATURE MARRIAGES

It would be unusual for a couple to maintain the intensity of romantic and erotic feelings that characterize the initial months of marriage. Gradually, the excitement of the relationship is replaced by every day concerns and tasks which are important to the ongoing maintenance of the relationship. The newness of the sexual experience diminishes, and the conversations which previously revealed interesting information become more directed to practical matters. Hopefully, romantic love becomes supplemented by a deeper sense of caring and appreciation as the couple share life situations together, and the marital bonding becomes a source of friendship, love, and intimacy.

Love

If there is any singular aspect to the feeling commonly described as mature love, it is acceptance. Loving, in its most developed form, involves the embracing of the loved person with a deeper appreciation and approval of that person just as they are. The bonding is cemented by the helpfulness and mutual maturing which each spouse renders to the other, with a deepening of appreciation and respectfulness of the other spouse's qualities and assets. It is an intuitive understanding and action of extending one's caring feelings to another, without expectations, or judgement, or evaluation. This is not an easy task even for the most mature of couples, for socialization in American society involves being shaped by messages of what is prized and what is valued and what is less worthy of our attention and appreciation, etc. Some individuals learn to be fearful of deeply accepting another because they feel that this might condone ways or qualities of being that are generally disapproved of by society. Furthermore, individuals mistakenly believe that the way to mature and improve themselves is to eliminate what they regard as their undesirable aspects and behaviors. They often are frightened of the process of opening up to, and accepting, aspects of themselves which they have judged unlovable. They fear that acceptance of these aspects will lead either to stagnation, or to an unwanted redefinition of themselves.

Intimacy

The foundation of intimacy is basic trust and communication. Basic trust is the experience of positiveness toward oneself and those close to us. It allows individuals to feel accepting of themselves and to value their loving feelings. This self-acceptance promotes a more relaxed psychological state of mind which makes for openness and allows couples to reach out toward each other with positive expectations of returned loving feelings. It diminishes unnecessary protectiveness and anticipation of hurts and rejections. This basic caring feeling toward oneself and others reduces the need to hide behind images, or to feel threatened that unacceptable aspects of ourselves will emerge. Out of this positiveness, communication flows more readily and couples allow themselves to be more "real." Where basic trust is present to a greater degree, partners are more mutually respectful of each other, and unrealistic expectations are minimized. As each partner more readily shares their feelings and difficulties, a better perspective of the needs and capabilities of each partner emerges.

Expectations and idealizations are a usual accompaniment of the courtship phase of a relationship. These expectations and idealizations derive from unresolved childhood dreams and needs which are then contributed to by one's partner, who is trying to put his/her best foot forward. As the relationship progresses and each person's idiosyncrasies, problems, and limitations become apparent, adjustments to each spouse's disappointed expectations become vital to sustaining and deepening loving feelings.

As stated earlier, a sustained loving relationship requires the deeper appreciation and acceptance of one's partner as they truly are, not as we expect them to be. This does not mean that if there are significant difficulties that problems cannot be addressed and changes hoped for; rather, it means that one starts to work on these problems with patience and an understanding of this is how things are rather than an attitude of, How can you be or act this way? Gurman (1978) believes that marital dysfunction can arise when the honeymoon is over, when the partners begin to sense the reality of who they married rather than seeing their mates through rose colored lenses.

DEVELOPMENTAL TASKS
AND EMOTIONAL MATURITY OR IMMATURITY

It is here that the role of individual personality dynamics is important in that they are powerful factors which relate to the couple's mutual capacity for happiness. It is the degree of nurturance, acceptance, appreciation, and sense of emotional security which the individuals experienced through their childhood emotional development that will largely contribute to how they respond to their spouse over time, and the level of intimacy that they will allow in the relationship. When we speak of levels of maturity, we are in fact, talking about the degree to which the person has been able or encouraged to develop their emotional and intellectual capabilities, along with a stabilized and positive sense of self. When there are blocks to this development such as in childhood situations of abandonment, abuse, neglect, or overindulgence, the person will display troubled personality dynamics.

By personality dynamics we mean the patterned sets of feelings, emotional reactions, and behaviors human beings exhibit as a result of their interaction with their environment and significant others. These patternings serve important functions of helping individuals anticipate and manipulate the environment to serve their needs, and to avoid pain, anxiety, or harm.

The human mind and brain functioning is established in such a way as to be able to shield from consciousness unwanted or painful aspects of feelings, thoughts, and experiences. This does not mean that they are inactive. It simply means that individuals can consciously carry on activities without distraction, more or less, from these unconscious elements. This state of affairs carries with it both major advantages and disadvantages. The major advantage is that persons are often spared the immediate pain or discomfort of feeling states which probably helps them to function more effectively in a current, immediate situation.

The major disadvantages are: (1) People are under the illusion that their conscious mental activity is the major source of their decision making functions, and that it represents the majority portion of what they would refer to as their mind or personality; (2) They do not understand that there are major aspects of their decisions and behaviors which emanate out of this unconscious reservoir of feelings and rejected aspects of themselves; (3) Feeling states which remain unconscious are free to play out in terms of substitutive behaviors which are not within awareness, or conscious choice. More importantly, however, the assumptions which are contained within these feeling states are beyond rational review. For example, if a young boy has a chronic experience of feeling unworthy because his mother is continuously unhappy, it would not be unusual for the child to blame himself for his mother's unhappiness. If he later goes on to repress this experience, the assumption which he made as a child that he must not have been loveable enough to make his mother happy remains in his unconscious unquestioned and accepted without reservation. He might therefore respond to the unhappiness in his spouse with discomfort and fear, unconsciously feeling that there must be something wrong with him because his wife is experiencing unhappiness and (4) When feeling states are unconscious, they assume the form of possessing non-logical properties. Parts can stand for wholes, and rules of orderly logic and understanding may not be applicable. The best example of non-logical or primary process thinking or feeling states is exemplified in dream states. Thus, if an aspect of our spouse's behavior reminds us unconsciously of a parent's personality or behavior, it is not uncommon for the piece of behavior to become representative of that individual as a whole evoking such reactions as "You're just like my mother!"

While each partner may have entered the marriage with a relatively stable personality, it is a recognized fact that longer term exposure to a troubled personality of one partner can adversely affect the personality structure of the other partner in important ways. As long as each partner is catering to the needs of the other partner, no matter how maladaptive, the couple will manage to function together and feel that the marriage is viable. As soon as one of the partners seeks a more healthy and permissive environment to develop more of their own personality, there is a significant threat to the relationship (Kaplan and Sadock, 1981). Pressure will be brought to bear on the partner by the less healthy individual to maintain the status quo. This situation is frequently encountered where one spouse is alcoholic. Despite the bitter complaints of the sober spouse about his/her mate's drinking, s/he nevertheless maintains a control of the relationship which endows him/her with esteem and power. When the alcoholic enters treatment and begins to make genuine changes in his/her personality and style of interaction, the mate may well sabotage treatment and subtly induce the spouse to resume drinking.

RELATIONSHIP TRAPS AND PITFALLS

There are many pitfalls along the way in the developmental transitions. One would think that being in a "loving relationship" would diminish the anxieties, or conversely, increase the trust, that people experience with one another. This is often not the case, however, as witnessed by the number of partnerships which deteriorate once the vows of marriage and commitment are exchanged. One of the main reasons for this is that the intimacy which marriage brings increases the threat of exposure or rejection which an individual may have feared through his/her life. The more important the spouse becomes, the greater the trauma anticipated should s/he be disapproved of or rejected by their partner.

Building Up Protective Mechanisms

The formation of the unconscious and the accompanying defense mechanisms which serve to protect our mental stability has been a topic which has been the basis of concern and exploration of various psychodynamic schools over the past 50 to 60 years. For a description of psychoanalytic thought as it relates to marital interactions, see Meissner (1978). While different psychodynamic orientations (Ackerman, 1958) have emphasized diverse feeling components as the basis for forming the need for repression and various defense mechanisms, psychoanalysts tend to agree that the unconscious together with the accompanying defense mechanisms for maintaining repression and the intactness of the unconscious are important determinants of overt human behavior (Sager, 1976).

The present authors support the view that one of the most important underlying motivational drives is the need for the individual to maintain a sense of security, diminished anxiety, and intact sense of self. This motivational system gives rise to the emphasis on the individual's need for self-protection which easily outweighs conscious considerations of love and romance when the individual feels him/herself to be in any way threatened. It is important to note though as Sager (1976) points out, defense or protective mechanisms are not necessarily pathological. If they do not become permanent ways of avoiding reality, they can have adaptive value. If, however, they cause distancing and/or excluding, they can lead to problems in a marriage.

Individuals' intellectual capacity to reason, anticipate, project, and analyze provides them with powerful tools to adapt and protect themselves. If they are accurate in their appraisal of the current situation and its potential problems or harms, then these processes serve them well. If, however, past wounds and sensitivities cause them to misinterpret present circumstances, then what was a positive asset now becomes a significant limitation, and they are likely to become defensive and emotionally restricted in the face of an anticipated unpleasantness, harm, or rejection. There are significant reasons for how these processes of misinterpretation develop which we will return to, but the main point to appreciate is that these personality dynamics are instrumental in whether the marital relationship will contain greater harmony or greater discord.

Protective measures are built up over a life time of experience and become incorporated into an individual's personality makeup. They are experienced by the person as a natural part of themselves, and more importantly, are felt to be a necessary part of their secure functioning. When these protective measures become more extreme, rigid, and inappropriate to the actual threats facing the individual, these defensive measures become maladaptive (Kolb and Brodie, 1982). Because these protective mechanisms are experienced by the individual as part of him/herself and necessary for survival, they are clung to with the belief that greater harm or threat will come if they are questioned or let go of. Because most of what individuals dislike about themselves and are rejected for by others is in reality their defensive maladaptive maneuvers, they are often in the paradoxical situation of suffering from the very same processes from which they are convinced they need to protect themselves. Indeed, individuals will not change despite their complaints of suffering or rejection until they can experientially understand that the way they are trying to defend against hurt and rejection is the major problem for them.

Painful or emotionally depriving experiences in childhood create a need to compensate for the effects they have had on self-esteem and feelings of self-worth. Individuals then develop expectations of self and others to offset these deprivations and handicaps to self-esteem and set about to fashion a self-image which excludes what is judged to be undesirable personality features. They long for the acceptance and unconditional love that would have been helpful in the past, and transfer these expectations onto the people who become most important in life. They think, "Surely if I am loved, those who love me will be willing and able to fulfill all my needs and expectations (Hendrix, 1989). In this way, they endow their partners with qualities and capabilities to help them accomplish this task only to later become disappointed and angry when they fall short of their expectations. Often, as a result of this process which may be acted out quite unconsciously, they become angriest and demand the most from those who are closest and most caring.

The need to protect oneself at all costs is most difficult for couples to understand because, for the most part, they are unaware of their underlying feelings. Security measures far outweigh the influence of romantic love which often contains within it idealizations and expectations by one's partner which can be frightening if the other partner is anxious or insecure. In order to avoid being a disappointment, a spouse might engage in what may appear to be destructive or unloving behavior which in reality are defensive maneuvers to avoid anticipated hurt.

There can be many types and degrees of protective measures invoked, as well as different vulnerabilities which are triggered by a marital relationship. Much to the puzzlement of many a spouse, these protective measures may only appear after a couple has formally entered into a marriage contract. People who have been living together for one to several years and then marry, may find an escalation of conflict in their relationship which did not exist while they were living together. The reality of a marriage contract, with its legal, economic, and emotional commitments is often frightening to an insecure partner who may feel trapped, or fearful that he/she will not be able to live up to the expectations of the agreement. S/he might feel the loss of an escape route should something "go wrong" in the relationship or may be frightened that s/he does not have the capacity to sustain a loving relationship. Or, s/he may mourn the loss of the opportunity to still have the option of pursuing other partners as a way of reassuring themselves that they are still desirable.

Another common factor in the formal marriage contract affecting the previously established live-in relationship is the fact that the spouse may have held off the expression of strong desires and preferences until s/he felt secure about the commitment. The more anxious partner frequently represses the awareness of these issues until pressured. The formalizing of the relationship then forces that partner to confront issues and feelings which were kept out of consciousness.

These patterns of behavior, with their attendant needs, expectations, frustrations, disappointments, and disillusionments, are powerful processes because they represent attempts by the person to repair hurts and wounds from the past. These hurts do not necessarily have to be traumatic events or devastating occurrences. They can be the day to day insensitivities and subtle lack of parental responsiveness which accumulate over time to undercut a child's confidence and positive feelings for life and appreciation of themselves.

While these reparative processes can become maladaptive when they are transferred intact onto a spouse, they nevertheless are attempts by that person to repair themselves and bring solace to their inner dis-ease. If that positive energy can be harnessed and redirected, that individual then has the opportunity to attempt that healing process with different tools.

In evolving defensive mechanisms to protect themselves, just as occurs in the process of worrying, individuals are attempting to anticipate, predict, and thus control a potentially threatening situation. Capacities for anticipation and prediction are dependent on memories of past experiences. When individuals recall past events and project them into the future in anticipation of trying to cope with what they feel is about to happen, they have a sense of power and control. They gear their forces up and feel a certain strength even if it means stirring up and holding onto negative feelings of anger, or hurt. If their estimation of the current situation and its similarity to past experiences is accurate, then the behavior is adaptive. If there are significant inaccuracies or misperceptions either about the present situation or the way things happened in the past, then they are susceptible to maladaptive behaviors.

One of the difficulties in this whole process of adaptation through anticipation and comparison with the past, is that the individual is dealing not only with factual events, but constellations of feelings, some or all of which may be unconscious, which alter the memory or understanding of these events. Therefore, not only are the actual recall of events open to error, but the understanding of the dynamics involved in these events may be faulty. As in our prior example, a mother's chronic unhappiness stemming from an unhappy marriage and personal conflicts can easily be erroneously experienced by a child as resulting from some fault of his in being able to make his mother happy. This set of experiences is then laid down in the child's memory and reproduced in his current feelings as they may apply to experiencing his spouse's unhappiness. Her distress may evoke anticipatory defensiveness in dealing with her unhappiness which may have little to do with him. This then might lead to his withdrawal of empathy, intensifying his wife's unhappiness.

Because so many crucial adaptive patterns and protections are formed in childhood, individuals are limited by the level of intellectual and emotional understanding that they possess as children. Further, childrens' developmental nature is to regard themselves as the center of their experience which could lead to a self-involved interpretation of events such as feeling that they are the cause or blame for occurrences. A frequent example of this situation occurs in situations of abuse and neglect, where the child feels responsible for the parent's behaviors. They are then locked into a pattern of anticipating abuse and trying desperately to figure out where they went wrong and what they can do to correct their deficiencies. This self-referential system also serves the adaptive function of giving the child some sense of control in feeling that there must be something s/he can do to repair and preserve the relationship with the parent. The acceptance of blame and guilt not only reinforces the sense of control, but preserves a relationship which would feel terrifying to be without. In accepting the blame, it is incomprehensible to a child to want to detach from an abusive parent, because if one's own parent is not caring, who else in the world would feel differently toward them (Chess and Hassibe, 1978; Klein, 1975)?

In the activation of these projective or anticipatory systems of defense, couples lose sight of the fact that they might be in error as to their past interpretations, and they may significantly underestimate the fact that as adults, they have developed capabilities and assets which could help them to react to a situation differently, if they remained open to it, before initiating defensive maneuvers.

If past hurts have been prominent, then the activation of these anticipatory defenses are most often involuntary. This set of circumstances leads to a situation where the individual repeatedly experiences negative outcomes of his/her behavior and is puzzled as to how this comes about. Because the defensive maneuvers are not within his/her consciousness, the person is unaware how the defensiveness may contribute to, or bring about the very results that they are trying to avoid. A common example is of a shy and insecure young man who attributes a considerable amount of the insecurity to the fact that women do not respond to him, when the more complete picture is that he will attend a party and relate only minimally, if at all, to the women at the party. His fear of anticipated rejection almost automatically evokes behaviors which cause him to remain on the periphery of activities, or to only have brief and awkward conversations with women he is introduced to.

Another significant difficulty with the anticipatory system of defense is the fact that partial similarities in the current situation are likely to trigger off stronger defensive reactions which were geared to more comprehensive dangers in the past. For example, a wife might have some similar characteristics to a husband's rejecting or controlling mother causing an unconscious major distancing maneuver because the part-identification unconsciously triggered a more global defensive reaction to an unconsciously perceived mother figure.

Defense Mechanisms

As individuals experience many aspects of life, there are always potentially conflicting or opposites aspects of situations. While people need a degree of protection in their lives through predictability based on the projection of past experiences onto current situations, this process is also very responsible for holding onto negative and painful experiences which not only continue the pain, but also the reinforcement of negative notions about themselves, and their experience of the world as a dangerous or threatening environment. Protective mechanisms that are typically used by couples are denial, projection, externalization and devaluation, and detachment. These defense mechanisms are employed by individuals in a marriage in order to avoid anticipated hurt or rejection.

Denial

Chief among these defenses is denial which allows persons not to attend to, and be actively aware of their behavior, expressions, or verbal communication which reveals the truer underlying aspects of their thoughts and feelings. They will disavow evidence which disputes their own consolidated view of themselves, fearing that any contradiction to their self-image will render them vulnerable to hurt, humiliation, or criticism. Denial allows for the addition of other mechanisms of defense such as projection, or externalization.

Projection

Projection is a fundamental process occurring out of a need for stability and protection which involves the transfer of inner states of mind or qualities onto the environment. The recipient of the transfer may either be a spouse or significant other, or the environment itself in the form of negative vibrations attached to a situation. Because repressed aspects of our life remain active and influential, even though they remain beyond every day awareness, projection is one mechanism to discharge the inner emotional tension that these unconscious aspects generate. In projection, the individual finds in others what s/he has been unable to accept in him/herself and can direct his/her energies to disparaging or criticizing others for these attributes. Other common means of discharging inner tension is through the pursuit of pleasure, sexuality, or mood altering substances such as drugs or alcohol.

Devaluation

Projection is often coupled with devaluation, which is the process of lowering the esteem or worth of the significant other by the projector, so as to avoid anticipated devaluation of oneself. By making the other less meaningful and valuable, any potential loss of that person is more easily borne, minimizing the risk of feeling loss, hurt, and rejection.

A detailed exploration of the varied defense mechanisms and their role in marital relationships is beyond the scope of this paper. However, it is helpful to address their main attributes:

1. Defenses frequently make their appearance in a more intensified way when intimacy deepens with its concomitant threat of rejection or abandonment in those individuals with underlying and significant emotional insecurities.
2. Defense mechanisms are necessary for normal adjustment but may become intensified leading to restricted and maladaptive behaviors and inner emotional suffering. Intensifications of defensive operations because of current precipitators may reactivate past vulnerabilities to the point where there is significant misinterpretation of present events.
3. Because defenses are replays of the past (anticipation and prediction foster reenactment of past emotional experiences), there are unconscious, accompanying belief systems which are themselves repressed and not accessible to rational processes. The individual is usually convinced s/he is operating under adult, rational processes and these processes are what make him/her who they are. Direct challenges to these beliefs, behaviors, or attitudes are frequently met with frustration, anger, or a feeling of being criticized.
4. These defenses create, for better or for worse, a stabilized sense of self which may be more or less realistic than the

individual appreciates, which may be a significant problem in intimate relationships where there is significant discrepancy between the actual and idealized self.

5. As the individual feels increasingly threatened, s/he tends to cling more to the defensive operations creating a vicious cycle of attack and defense with the spouse. This conflict leads to a confusion of what the truer nature of the actual here and now problem between the couple actually is, as opposed to reactivation of premarital emotional problems.

6. When defensive operations are more intensely mobilized, persons become hyper-focused on the current triggers of their sense of being threatened or hurt by their spouse, and so, have a much diminished awareness that the hurt and threat they are currently experiencing derives from a more fundamental, and relevant set of past experiences. Indeed, the current interaction or trigger may only represent a smaller part of their underlying vulnerability with its accompanying hurt and pain.

7. Because defenses are ubiquitous in personality makeup, it is easy for each spouse to cite the defenses of their partner as being responsible for the conflict, and avoid appreciating how each partner is contributing to the conflict.

There are many strategies for engaging and assisting marital conflict brought about in some measure by defensive operations triggered by the underlying emotional vulnerabilities of one or both of the partners. Given the aforementioned factors in defensive maneuvers, we have found it helpful to bring the couple together in an atmosphere of patience, acceptance, and non-critical observation of what is transpiring at the individual and couple level. This exploration fosters a mutual search of themselves as individuals as well as a couple so as to reduce the fear of being real, and communicative of truer thoughts and feelings with reduced threat of criticism and rejection. When people come to understand that their misperceptions, maladaptive behaviors, and objectionable aspects of their personalities are understandable past attempts to cope and adapt, they are able to accept emotional correction more easily, and bring a compassion and empathy to the arena which is healing to both themselves and their spouse. It makes more sense to couples when they can experience that they are reliving past hurts and vulnerabilities, and rather than being labeled as "crazy" or "unreasonable," they now understand how their past needs to protect themselves account for what appears to be unreasonable behavior.

Marriages which have a foundation of health will be able to withstand these revelations of the truer nature of their spouses and will grow from the experience of openness and realness in the relationship. It is the defensive operations which account for the problems more than the feelings themselves.

A frequent experience in couple's arguments is to have a surprised spouse who has been just accused of various types of behavior answer with an unbelievable "but that's just the way you are!" The process of projection blinds couples to those qualities within themselves which they find objectionable. They are then less able to identify them and accept them as parts of themselves so as to bring meaningful help to themselves rather than to become condemnatory.

CASE MATERIAL

After the breakup of his first marriage, Jack finally remet and married a woman he had known in his teenage years. He had idolized her as a youth and felt he would never be deserving enough to be loved by her. Following a whirlwind courtship in which some of his confidence was bolstered by alcohol, Jack became increasingly frightened that his wife would not think him manly enough. Over the ensuing years, he began to exhibit a belligerence and need for control which undercut the joy of the initial years of the marriage. His sense of insecurity, which he dared not share with Louise less she think less of him, began to manifest itself sexually in terms of premature ejaculation. Louise was puzzled and dismayed at the turn their marriage was taking. She felt unattractive to Jack and felt he was losing his respect and love for her. In view of his controlling and dominating demeanor as well as his business success, she didn't understand his behavior as representing anxiety and insecurity. Jack's emotionally troubled background, in which he felt be-

littled and humiliated by his father and ignored by his mother, made him suspicious that he could be genuinely loved and respected.

The above example is an instance in which one partner was experiencing significant anxieties stemming from inner feelings of insecurity and inadequacy which resulted from childhood experiences. These anxieties created a need to protect himself in the growing intimacy with his wife, who was fast becoming a potential threat. The history of this couple's difficulties is by no means uncommon in terms of a clear understanding and sharing of what their problems were. Louise had little notion of Jack's inner insecurities and Jack was unable to identify and admit his anxieties to Louise. Their arguments came to be focused on realistic but superficial issues which engaged their attention to the point where both had little awareness of the more troubling aspects of their relationship. Nadelson (1978) discusses therapeutic techniques for assessing the role of early childhood issues in a couple's marital functioning.

Jack's significant childhood and adolescent emotional experiences sensitized him to the point where he maintained his defenses even in the face of Louise's appeals for mutual love and respect, and despite the fact that his behavior was jeopardizing the marriage. His fear of exposure and expected humiliation by her made him cling steadfastly to his perceptions of the situation in which he felt his wife was disrespectful of him and did not care for him the way she had when they were engaged.

For her part, Louise could not understand what happened to their initial loving relationship and felt that if he truly loved her, he would listen to her distress and change. In the face of the couple's continued problems, Louise was easily able to accept blame and responsibility for the problems in their marriage. This stemmed historically from her critical father who consistently berated her. In this way, she learned to perceive herself as less desirable and worthy as a person, and later as a wife. She had little understanding of her own unconscious processes or of the inner emotional anxieties which Jack experienced. In their own unique way they colluded (Willi, 1982) helping her to maintain a sense of stability and continuity with past definitions of herself and helping him to maintain his defensiveness.

Jack's personality problems reflect an over-preoccupation with the self, an overestimation of personal qualities, and unrealistic expectations of the self. This over evaluation is a compensation for underlying feelings of low self-esteem, and often, fears of abandonment. Problems similar to Jack's and Louise's type may not make their significant appearance until specific stresses or intimacy develops making it difficult for the intended spouse to be prepared. If soft signs of emotional personality problems do make their appearance during courtship, the intended spouse is likely to dismiss them as idiosyncratic, or behavior which they believe will change as their love deepens. The goal of therapy here involved a restructuring of both Jack's and Louise's internally based perceptions and expectations of each other. The primary goal was to deal with the aspects of each partner's personality that was specifically important to the marital relationship. This was accomplished through a sharing of each others' present and past experiences of pain and crises. First there was the use of "I" statements to convey feelings in the present, "I feel hurt when you . . . "; next these feelings were validated by the spouse, "When I do . . . , you feel hurt"; and finally, these feelings were expressed in a historical context, "I used to feel these same kinds of feelings when . . . " In so doing, the couple became more empathic and supportive of each other. With Jack and Louise, this eventually led to a renewal of their original marital commitment to each other. During the therapeutic process, the couple learned about the role of their historically based unconscious processes on their marital relationship. In this way, they and their therapist were able to systemically diagnose, assess, and explore their marital relationship while also examining the linear links to the past.

REFERENCES

Ackerman, N. (1958). *The psychodynamics of everyday life*. New York: Basic Books.
Blanck, R. and Blanck, G. (1968). *Marriage and personal development*. New York: Columbia University Press.
Chess, S. and Hassibi, M. (1978). *Principles and practice of child psychiatry*. New York: Plenum Press.
Gurman, A.S. (1985). Contemporary Marital Therapies: A critique and comparison of psychoanalytic, behavioral, and systems theory approaches. In T. Paoli-

no, Jr. and B. McCrady (Eds.), *Marriage and Marital Therapy*. New York: Brunner/Mazel.

Hendrix, H. (1988). *Getting the love that you want*. New York:Harper and Row.

Kaplan, H. and Sadock, B. (1981). *Modern synopsis of comprehensive textbook of psychiatry III*. 3rd Ed. Baltimore, MD: Waverly Press.

Klein, M. (1975). *The psychoanalysis of children*. New York: Delacorte Press.

Kolb, L. and Brodie, H. (1982). *Modern clinical psychiatry*. New York: W.B. Saunders and Co.

Mahler, M. (1975). *The psychological birth of the human infant*. New York: Basic Books.

Martin, P. (1976). *A marital therapy manual*. New York: Brunner/Mazel.

Meissner, W. (1978). The conceptualization of marriage and family dynamics from a psychoanalytic perspective. In T. Paolino, Jr. and B. McCrady (Eds.), *Marriage and marital therapy*. New York: Brunner/Mazel.

Nadelson, C. (1978). Marital therapy from a psychoanalytic perspective. In T. Paolino, Jr. and B. McCrady (Eds.), *Marriage and marital therapy*. New York: Brunner/Mazel.

Sager, C. (1976). *Marriage contracts and couple therapy*. New York: Brunner/Mazel.

Willi, J. (1982). *Couples in collusion*. New York: Aronson.

Response to Lawrence Maltin
and Joan D. Atwood's Article:
"The Tasks and Traps of Relationships"

Pauline Rose Clance

The author does a good job of clearly, accurately and simply stating the major tasks of relationship building and the traps that derail and harm relationships. If a couple can agree on the seven developmental tasks as fundamental and important, there is a great possibility they can overcome difficulties. I find some of the most difficult work occurs at the fundamental level in which one of the couple does not believe in equality and respect. Gender differences often occur as couples struggle with the tasks of creating a healthy relationship.

The traps and pitfalls in developing intimacy are covered from the perspective of the therapist or through the eyes of the therapist. If the therapist can get the couple intrigued with and fascinated in the defenses and their processes, connection rather than disconnection becomes possible. The author presents the traps in a straightforward, cognitive manner yet they are experienced by the couple in an affective, emotional manner. One must help them gain some emotional hope before they are able to look at their terror and defensiveness. How to interrupt a vicious cycle between them is often difficult and touchy and depends on many, many factors. As I approach a couple, I have great trepidation as to whether I will have the knowledge and the skill to do so–to create a space for them to regain perspective.

Pauline Rose Clance, PhD, is a board member with *Journal of Couples Therapy* and is also affiliated with Georgia State University, University Plaza, Atlanta, GA 30303.

133

Certainly the tasks and traps of relationship building as discussed by Joan Atwood could be applied to bigger systems. The same fundamental tasks of communication and relating occur at the agency level, the community, state, national and international level. Defensiveness and lack of communication lead to vicious cycles at all these levels.

If we can learn to disrupt vicious cycles of attack and defensiveness at the family level, we may be able to use that knowledge to work for healing between diverse, large systems.

If there is to be love and connection in the world, then I must create love and connections with those nearest me in the here and now. I find I am able to do so powerfully at moments and that other times I fail miserably and that I have to pick myself up, dust myself off, have some self empathy or understanding from another and begin all over again.

I think we must individually and as a nation know in our cells that war is not an acceptable alternative. We must begin to put our resources into learning about health and healing rather than into creating instruments of destruction.

To long for communication, intimacy and connection is an important step. As intimate systems therapists, I think we are committed to the possibility that people can learn to live together in ways that enhance rather than destroy vitality and life.

Each time I see an individual, a couple, family or group, I commit myself hour to hour to the possibility that positive connection is possible.

Couples Therapy
from a Systems Perspective

Dorothy S. Becvar
Raphael J. Becvar

SUMMARY. A systemic framework for understanding the dynamics of couple interaction and for working with couples in therapy is delineated. This theoretical model, which focuses on relationships, is illustrated concretely by means of case vignettes. It is asserted that therapy from a systems perspective is particularly useful when working with couples; that although not necessarily pleasant, warring behavior has meaning; and that connectedness is inevitable and therefore disconnectedness is a matter of degree.

Couples therapy offers a unique opportunity to utilize a systemic approach. Conversely, this approach is ideally suited to working with couples in general, and with warring couples, in particular. For, it provides a model for understanding the way that human beings connect with or disconnect from one another; a framework for delineating the specifics of therapeutic ways of dealing with warring couples; a perspective from which to view the effects such warring has on couples; and a means of explaining the critical dynamics behind the shift from warring to loving relationships, and vice versa. In this article we therefore delineate the metaperspective of systems theory as a way of understanding both couple dynamics and therapeutic interaction. This skeleton is given flesh by means of case vignettes which are interspersed throughout.

Dorothy S. Becvar, PhD, is affiliated with Washington University.
Raphael J. Becvar, PhD, is affiliated with St. Louis Family Institute.
Their address is GWB School of Social Work, Washington University, Campus Box 1196, Brown Hall, St. Louis, MO 63130.

From the perspective of systems theory at the level of simple cybernetics (Keeney, 1983), the focus of therapy is relational and contextual whether the client is an individual, a couple or a family. Thus we are moved to a consideration of the dynamics of interaction between individuals and the redundant patterns which are characteristic of their relationships. We understand a complementarity in the behaviors of each member of a relationship relative to the other, regardless of whether the behaviors are experienced positively or negatively. The behaviors fit and from them may be inferred the rules that have been negotiated, either overtly or covertly, for that relationship. Such rules are an expression of the way in which members of a couple connect with each other.

Amy and Bill have been married for twenty years. Bill discounts and ignores Amy's feelings and verbal requests, treating her like a child. Amy wants peace at any price and has a long history of swallowing her anger at Bill's behavior. Instead, she soothes her ruffled feathers by spending a great deal of money on clothes and other items for herself. This spending behavior infuriates Bill and fuels his belief that she is childlike.

When working with a warring couple such as Amy and Bill, a systems perspective enables us to avoid the pitfall of triangulation through either taking sides or sharing secrets with one member or the other. Though it is possible to see Bill as the "heavy," we are aware that he can only continue to ignore or discount Amy as long as she continues to accept this behavior rather than risking open warfare. Refusing to take sides also requires that we explain to both that we reserve the right to insist that any information shared privately by one or the other be available for open discussion by all if that is deemed therapeutically appropriate. For, our "client" is the relationship and we understand that each member has contributed to its creation, no matter how painful it feels. Thus, we also do not place blame, operating instead out of an epistemology of participation (Becvar & Becvar, 1988).

That is, from the perspective of higher order systems theory, or cybernetics of cybernetics (Keeney, 1983), all human interaction may be described as a process of structural coupling (Maturana, 1978). Thus, "organisms survive by fitting with one another and with other aspects of their context" (Becvar & Becvar, 1988, p. 80).

Accordingly, interactions have meaning in a given context and describe a recursive process of mutual influence, feedback and adaptation within a range determined by the respective structure of each individual.

Structure, in this instance, is derived from a combination of heredity and experience and refers to beliefs, or perceptual frameworks, according to which information is processed, meaning is ascribed and reality is thereby constructed. Indeed, systems are said to be structurally determined, i.e., they are limited in their responses to that which their structure allows (Maturana, 1974). Further, the structure of a system exists as a function of its previous and ongoing recursive processes of mutual influence, feedback and adaptation.

Carol and Don have also been together for many years. Don perceives Carol as critical and judgmental, basing much of his opinion on Carol's nonverbal behaviors, which are similar to those he observed in his mother. Carol feels Don is mindreading and resents the fact that Don "overreacts" to what she describes as an expressive face, which is "just a part of who she is." They fight their battles quietly as Don withdraws into work and Carol recoils from any attempts at physical intimacy.

Over the years our warring couples have evolved a way to be with each other which, if nothing else, is predictable. The battles in which they engage are part of the fabric of their relationship; they allow the couples to define who each member is with the other and are part of the process by means of which their stability is maintained. Further, the conflict which such couples experience can be viewed as a form of intimacy as surely as that of a couple whose behavior we would describe as loving.

In other words, warring has meaning beyond the obvious experience of hostility. One must therefore be careful when judging the effects that warring has on the couple. For, while at the level of content such behavior may appear and feel negative, at the level of process it has its positive aspects. Similarly, one must also be careful when proceeding to facilitate change. Some questions we may wish to pose for a couple's consideration, therefore, include the following: Will you know who you are and how to behave with each other if you are no longer fighting? Who else in the family will be affected by such a drastic change and what will its impact be? Do you really want to become vulnerable and risk being intimate in a more loving way? Is the instability that accompanies the process of change worth the potential benefits? Such questions may have the feel of a therapeutic paradox, or restraint from change. At the same time, however, given a systems perspective they are straightforward questions in that the desired change may indeed have unforeseeable ramifications.

That is, the model for change consistent with a systems perspective is the flip side of our description of the way in which redundant patterns of interaction evolve and thus stability is maintained (Watzlawick, Weakland & Fisch, 1974). It provides us with a way to understand the critical dynamics behind the shift from warring to loving relationships. Accordingly, change requires a change in the context relative to which behaviors have meaning. It can therefore be difficult to achieve and is not necessarily experienced positively despite its having been desired. Thus it is our belief that when clients come in for therapy, they are simultaneously requesting both that we help them to change and that we allow them to remain the same.

Emily and Frank have been in and out of therapy for years in an effort to heal their relationship. Problems in their marriage began to surface when Emily decided to return to school to prepare for a professional career about the time that their children entered adolescence. Although Frank declared his support of women's liberation in general and Emily's choice in particular, his vision of marriage was based on a more traditional model. Emily, on the other hand, had built up a great store of resentment towards Frank based on behaviors derived from living according to a traditional model of marriage. Although each strongly professed a desire and a willingness to change, and made seemingly valiant attempts toward that end, ultimately one or the other would sabotage any new behaviors and life would return to the previously established status quo. The implicit message was that they really did not want to stay married to each other, and ultimately they decided upon a divorce.

What occurred with Emily and Frank might be described as first-order change when what was needed was second-order change (Watzlawick et al., 1974). That is, while change occurred within the system, there was no change of the system. The context remained the same as Emily continued to resent Frank and Frank continued to act out his displeasure with Emily's desire to rewrite the rules for their relationship. While both made efforts to behave differently, the same basic patterns were maintained.

On the other hand, second-order change occurs when the rules of the relationship change, changes in perceptions occur and thus new behavioral alternatives become available. The classic example is that which occurs with the successful use of a reframe. With a reframe a problem situation is lifted out of its old context, or set or rules, and is placed in a new context, with new rules, which defines it equally as well. Alternative understanding, or a new meaning, emerges as a function of the new context and thus new and different responses become not only logical but possible. We might compare this with the shift in our view which occurs when we take a photograph out of its old, dark frame and place it in a new lighter frame. We literally get a new perspective and begin to see things differently than we did before.

Gail and Harry came to therapy complaining about their roller coaster relationship. Each was quite successful in related careers, they had a nice home, took vacations together from time to time and genuinely seemed to like each other. However, they had a recurring pattern of fighting followed by silent withdrawal followed by a truce and peace-making followed by intimacy and love-making followed by fighting, and on and on. Because both professed to love each other very much they were puzzled by the periods of fighting and eager for them to end. Rather than agreeing that the fights were bad, part of the therapeutic process included reframing these periods of conflict as an important mechanism for getting some needed distance when things got too close for comfort. Whether or not this was actually the case, it was an acceptable explanation for Gail and Harry and opened the door to a consideration of alternative, less hurtful ways to create spaces in their togetherness.

In order for a reframe to be successful, however, it must be acceptable and believable by the client. As noted in our discussion of structural coupling, there is a fit between the behaviors of each member of a relationship, whether we are talking about the couple or the therapist and the client. To be effective, the client/therapist relationship must be characterized by a fit which may be described as one in which the channel the therapist is using to transmit is the same channel that the client is using to receive. Thus the specifics of therapeutic ways of dealing with warring couples include a need to have knowledge of the beliefs, or perceptual frame, according to which their context is defined. That is, the same reframe as the one described above is likely to make little or no sense to a couple who understand the world in more concrete terms and who would therefore have difficulty buying such an abstract construction of their reality.

Indeed, successful therapeutic intervention must be an embodiment of what Keeney (1983) calls "meaningful noise." Therefore, in addition to being acceptable and believable, one's strategies must also represent a source of the random, or something new, to draw upon (Varela, 1981). We like to think of couples who come to therapy as being stuck and in need of new information in order to get unstuck. Generally they have been trying for a long time to solve their problem. However, not only have their attempted solutions not worked, they have become part of the problem, i.e., part of the pattern within which the problem is being maintained (Watzlawick et al., 1974). They are literally spinning their wheels. We therefore see our job as one of sprinkling some sand on the mud in which they are mired so that they can move out of their rut and experience the freedom of a return to the open road. The "sand" is the new information, or noise, aspect of our intervention which facilitates a change in context. It is meaningful in that the use of sand makes sense when one is stuck in the mud.

As noted previously, real change is not necessarily a comfortable experience, for it is usually accompanied by a period of instability. As new rules evolve and the system is thus changed there is a loss of predictability and a sense of insecurity as each member attempts to let go of the old and become comfortable with the new. A strategy for dealing with this phenomenon is to predict it, thereby creating a therapeutic paradox. This may be done either through a straight explanation, as above, or by means of metaphor.

For example, during the first session with a couple it is often useful to give a homework assignment. One of our favorites is to ask the couple to spend fifteen minutes a day with each other doing something enjoyable. They are not to discuss their problems and, as much as possible, there are to be no interruptions. Though such an assignment seems easy enough and probably even desirable, we know from experience that it may really challenge the couple. We therefore predict that they might not either be able to or choose to do it (paradox #1). Further, we warn them that if they do choose to follow our suggestions they will probably feel uncomfortable (paradox #2). For doing different behaviors is likely to feel similar to the experience of being in a boat with someone and deciding to change seats. While each is moving about and finding a new place to sit, the boat will undoubtedly rock a great deal. The rocking will continue until each finds a comfortable place once again and a new balance is achieved.

The essence of a therapeutic paradox is thus to predict or request behavior or feelings that ordinarily occur spontaneously. By making a prediction or request for such behaviors or feelings, their occurrence is less likely, which is a plus. And if they do occur, we have predicted or requested that they would, hence we are in a no-lose situation.

Homework assignments can therefore be a very useful tool in couples therapy. They are a means for perturbing the system and give us a great deal of information about whether the couple chooses to follow through or not and in what way. In addition, we are also aware that, in our efforts to facilitate change, if we take something away, it is important to put something back in. In other words, if a couple stops fighting, they need to have something else they can do with each other. Conversely, creating a situation in which new, more satisfactory behaviors are experienced may preclude some old, less desirable behaviors.

Irene and Jack have been married for five years. Both had been married previously and Irene has full custody of the two adolescent children from her previous marriage. While Irene and Jack get along well in most areas, how the children should be reared had been a very volatile issue. Because Jack is a step-parent, we recommended that he back out of the parenting role, disciplining only on authority borrowed from Irene. While they could certainly discuss together how to deal with the children, Irene, as the natural mother, was to be in charge of implementing rules and handling discipline. Knowing that Jack would thus lose an important role in the family, we suggested that he take on the new role of friend to the children, which was available to him since he was not their biological parent. Despite initial discomfort on all sides, the battles between Irene and Jack ceased and a new, more loving context evolved.

While this intervention was based on knowledge derived from research with step-parent families (Visher & Visher, 1988), we believe that the most any information about individuals, couples or families can provide is a story which may or may not be useful. That is, from a systemic perspective, we construct our reality and the observer is part of the observed (Segal, 1986). Subjectivity is inevitable and we always influence our research findings, no matter how rigorous our methodology. Both clinical and empirical research, therefore, provide us with theories, and for theory, we substitute the word story. Therapy thus becomes a process of "storying" our clients in a way that facilitates change. And dealing with each unique couple or client system will require the creation of a story which accommodates that uniqueness. Indeed, this is part of the process of making our noise meaningful and thus increasing the probability of success.

Despite our best efforts, however, the fact is that many couples will opt to end their relationship or divorce. As was the case with Emily and Fred, the couple is now faced with the challenge of disconnecting. From a systems perspective we become aware that what this really means is that they must renegotiate their relationship, particularly if children are involved. For as long as they must interact with each other, they are in relationship and they are connected. And if the same old patterns continue to repeat, we cannot say that the marriage has ended regardless of the fact that there is a legal document that says they are divorced.

Karen and Larry have been divorced for three years. Neither has remarried, although Larry is involved in a new relationship. Karen has custody of their two children and Larry has liberal visitation rights which he exercises conscientiously. Both were satisfied with their financial agreement and neither has suffered a significant change in lifestyle. Larry wanted the divorce because he saw Karen as a controlling woman. Karen complained about Larry's passive aggressive behavior and his failure to let her know that he was unhappy. Today this couple's power struggle continues to be played out around child care arrangements, with Larry complaining that Karen is trying to run his life and dictate who he can and cannot see. Karen is furious at Larry's secretive behavior and spends a great deal of energy analyzing both their marriage and Larry's personality. As long as they engage in the same old warring ways, the divorce is just a technicality.

With divorcing couples who have children, the renegotiation process can sometimes be facilitated around the goal of learning how to co-parent now that the former spouses are no longer a couple. For this provides each with the opportunity to set aside their differences and focus on what is best for the children. A related goal is the need to build a new life not only for the sake of the children but also for the good of the parent. A useful story here is that the better the parent takes care of him/herself, the better job s/he will do as a single parent.

When helping childless couples to disconnect, we focus on such things as the amount of power that is given away when the entire focus of our life is anger at the ex-spouse. We also mention an irony in what may happen when the members of the couple begin to rebuild their lives. On the one hand, as one learns to enjoy life again and have new interests one is better equipped to establish a new relationship out of desire rather than out of need. On the other hand, if there is any hope at all of the couple ever getting back together again it is at the point of feeling good about oneself that this is most likely to happen. Once again, this is a win-win prescription, both for the therapist and for the client.

Systemic therapy thus enables us to capture the dance in which each of us participates as we move into and out of relationships. For life, according to this story, is a process of coupling and we are always connected. What changes is the degree to which we are connected and the way that connection is experienced. Some conflict is inevitable, or as an old friend of ours used to say, "You aren't dancing very close together if you never step on each other's toes." And while making love is undoubtedly more enjoyable than making war, warring is at least an expression of connectedness. Indeed, reality from a systems perspective is relational and the key to understanding is "the pattern which connects" (Bateson, 1979).

REFERENCES

Bateson, G. (1979). *Mind and nature.* New York: E. P. Dutton.

Becvar, D. S. & Becvar, R. J. (1988). *Family therapy: A systemic integration.* Boston, MA: Allyn & Bacon.

Keeney, B. P. (1983). *Aesthetics of change.* New York: Guilford Press.

Maturana, H. (1974). Cognitive strategies. In H. Von Foerster (Ed.), *Cybernetics of cybernetics* (pp. 457-469). Urbana IL: University of Illinois.

Maturana, H. (1978). Biology of language: The epistemology of reality. In G. A. Miller & E. Lennerberg (Eds.), *Psychology and biology of language and thought: Essays in honor of Eric Lennerberg* (pp. 27-63). New York: Academic Press.

Segal, L. (1986). *The dream of reality.* New York: W. W. Norton.

Varela, F. J. (1981). Introduction. In H. Von Foerster, *Observing systems* (pp. xi-xvi). Seaside, CA: Intersystems Publications.

Visher, E. B. & Visher, J. S. (1988). *Old loyalties, new ties: Therapeutic strategies with stepfamilies.* New York: Brunner/Mazel.

Watzlawick, P., Weakland, J. & Fisch, R. (1974). *Change.* New York: W. W. Norton.

Comment–
Response to Dorothy S. Becvar and Raphael J. Becvar's Article: "Couples Therapy from a Systems Perspective"

Sam Kirschner
Diana Adile Kirschner

"Couples Therapy from a Systems Perspective" provides a lovely overview of the basic tenets of the systems approach to couples therapy. An important aspect of that viewpoint is that marital conflict represents a kind of connection or intimacy between the partners which helps maintain stability. Therapy, therefore, must respect the fact that couples want to both change and stay the same.

The systemic description of couples interactions is a useful way to understand the homeostatic patterns and role allocations which tie up distressed couples in knots. But is it a sufficient explanation? And, more importantly, does it inform us as to what techniques are useful in creating change? The Becvars, themselves, note in their book, *Family Therapy: A Systemic Integration* (1988), "Systems theory is not a pragmatic theory" (p. 12). They go on to say that the systems view does not tell the clinician which strategies and techniques are effective with which specific problems. As most experienced couples therapists have come to appreciate, a truly pragmatic approach usually includes a wide variety of methodologies and strategies. This is because the problems of couples are multi-deter-

Sam Kirschner and Diana Adile Kirschner are both *Journal of Couples Therapy* board members. Correspondence may be addressed to them at 1615 Kings Mill Road, PO Box 448, Gwynedd Valley, PA 19437.

mined. They include: the interactional dynamics in the here and now, the couple's history, and each partner's cognitive, emotional and behavioral functioning.

The systemic view, on the other hand, entirely ignores the importance of dealing with each partner's history, issues and difficulties, even though they often shape and influence the systemic functioning of the couple. For example, what if one member of a couple is manic-depressive? What if the wife is being beaten? Should we ignore these phenomena as being secondary to the systemic considerations? What if one of the partners is a survivor of incest or physical abuse? What if the husband is an alcoholic or comes from an alcoholic family? All of these conditions strongly affect the relationship.

If a member of a couple is suffering from a severe depression, or from the traumatic aftereffects of childhood physical or sexual abuse, he or she may be unable to move into a more loving and intimate relationship despite any systemic intervention. When these types of individual problems are not addressed, they can subvert or undo even the most clever strategic techniques. In order to prevent this, the depressed partner may need to be put on appropriate medication, and the "traumatized" partner may need individual sessions to deal with the wounds of the past.

In our work, we have integrated individual and marital therapy along with systemic work (Kirschner & Kirschner, 1986) because we have found that individual therapy is typically required for successful treatment outcome in 90% of our marital cases. Only those couples who enter treatment with a great deal of psychological health, in which both partners have mature egos and a willingness to take responsibility for creating a positive relationship can benefit from only conjoint sessions. The large majority of clients are not in this category. Rather they have suffered from various gaps, deficiencies and traumas in their families of origin. They often have had no role models for intimate relating and have experienced great disappointment in love relationships in the past. Therefore, creating more lasting second order changes usually requires individual as well as conjoint sessions. Ideally, the two need to be artfully woven together for maximum clinical effectiveness.

All of the cases mentioned in the article raise questions about the lack of importance placed on the individual work. Perhaps Emily and Frank would not have divorced if they each had had a chance to work through and heal the wounds of the past. In the case of Amy and Bill, does Amy suffer from low self-esteem and an inability to assert herself or fight constructively? Does she need corrective individual sessions in which she experiences herself, her thoughts and feelings as important or learn to assert herself before she could even begin to get closer to Bill? Is Bill from an alcoholic family? Is his controlling, parentified stance an outgrowth of severe deficits in trust which he developed in an alcoholic system? What are his fears, his fantasies regarding "letting go"? If these issues are not explored and worked through, it would be very hard for Bill to change his role in the couple.

Similarly, in the case of Don and Carol, is Carol an incest victim? Perhaps she is warding off repressed memories of incestuous activities, and this process impedes her ability to have a physical relationship with Don. Does Don have deep fears of annihilation as a result of physical abuse which he suffered as a child? If so, he will continue to unconsciously orchestrate the physical distance in the relationship unless these fears are addressed and perhaps treated with desensitization techniques.

In sum, the systemic view is a powerful way of understanding the relationship patterns of couples in conflict. Equally as important, however, is understanding each partner's cognitive, emotional, and behavioral dynamics. And more important than both is knowing when to focus on the individual or the couple and what techniques to use with which problem.

REFERENCES

Becvar, D.S. & Becvar, R.J. (1988). *Family therapy: A systemic integration.* Boston, MA: Allyn & Bacon.

Kirschner, D.A. & Kirschner, S. (1986). *Comprehensive family therapy: An integration of systemic and psychodynamic treatment models.* New York, NY: Brunner/Mazel.

WHAT OUGHT TO BE THE RESPONSIBLE PSYCHOTHERAPIST'S ATTITUDE RELATIVE TO WAR?

The question I posed myself on the launching of the Persian Gulf War, so alien to my own beliefs about productive conflict resolution: What ought to be the responsible psychotherapist's attitude relative to war and to this particular war?

Part of my answer, in addition to development of the theme for this volume, was the circulation–among several colleagues across the country–of my editorial, "Ask Not for Whom the Siren Wails"; it appeared in *Coupling . . . What Makes Permanence,* which was being assembled at the time the war was launched. The following comments by Schell and Cole are responses.

–Barbara Jo Brothers

"Interbe":
Comment on "Ask Not for Whom the Siren Wails"

Bruce Schell

The following emerged in response to Brothers' (1991) article. A central thread was the crucial importance of recognizing the essential humanness of all of us coupled with the importance of fostering our growth as individuals and as psychotherapists in becoming "more fully human." The backdrop to that theme was its alternative war, the consequence of our shift from an I-thou relationship with the world to an I-it relationship with the world.

"Will you love me?"
"Dare I love you?"
"Can I trust that you love me?"
"Will you accept my love?"

The list could go on and on for matters of the heart are central to our lives. It is inherent in our nature that we yearn to love and be loved. Intimacy and love are basic needs present from the moment of our conception. Yet, the news media are not filled with stories of the many facets of love, rather they are replete with stories of wars, murders, and betrayals. A way of understanding that is provided by Lowen's (1980) idea that striving for power is all that is left when you have given up the hope of ever being loved and valued. Shocking support for that is given in an article by Lewis et al. (1988)

Bruce Schell, PhD, is Clinical Psychologist and Professor, Department of Family and Preventive Medicine, University of South Carolina School of Medicine, Columbia, SC 29201.

151

investigating adolescents convicted and condemned to die for capital crimes (murder). The article investigated the history of these violent criminals (adolescent children). Their crimes had occurred when they were between fifteen and seventeen years of age. The majority had been brutally physically abused including being burned, whipped, stomped, and beaten or kicked in the head. The majority had serious neurological abnormalities related to brain injuries. A third had been sexually abused by one or more individuals. Not only had their hope for love been lost to be replaced by the most primitive exercise of power, but people were now objects, things to be feared, hated, and destroyed. The temptation is to view these murderers (adolescent children) as evil creatures and in turn make them objects for us to destroy or lock away from sight. By making them objects we can attempt to avoid seeing that, but for a turn of fate and circumstance they are our children or us. This same process by which we are tempted to turn them into objects is the one we use to turn nation states into "the other." It has been a maxim of psychotherapy theories that we all contain within us all aspects of humanity. In nascent form or actualized we are noble, evil, generous, cruel and every other conceivable trait of the species. In making the adolescent murderers objects we distance the truth of our own woundings and of the consequences of those early internalized messages that cripple our ability to see each other and our ability to respond to each other out of the compassionate aspects of our nature. We have spent the last four and a half decades with a defined evil, the Soviet Union, to project on our own lack of humanity. With the end of the "evil empire" we may either accept all aspects of our own nature or we are doomed as a nation to an endless crusade to rid the world of our own projections. It seems time for us to learn and then to teach what is expressed in Thich Nhat Hanh's (1987) words that "we all interbe": that we are interpenetrating, interdependent with all sentient life. This truth is obscured by our wounds and internalized messages. If as psychotherapists we receive enough psychotherapy that our wounds are healed and enough personal growth that we can be our "best human being" then in our encounters with others we begin to quicken in them their greater possibilities.

The process whereby I make my partner an object upon which I project my disowned parts is the same process whereby I make the feared "other" of ethnic groups or of nation states. It rests upon my fearful turning away from my own internal world and thereby remaining ignorant of my own shadow. The more I cleave to the truth that we all interbe and hold fast to our common humanity the more successfully we will all make love, not war at the micro and macro level.

REFERENCES

Brothers, B. (1991). Ask not for whom the siren wails. *Journal of couples therapy* 2(3), 11-16.

Hanh, Thich Nhat (1987). *Being peace*. Berkeley: Parallax Press.

Lewis, D. et al. (1988). Neuropsychiatric, psychoeducational and family characteristics of 14 juveniles condemned to death in the United States. *American Journal of psychiatry* 145(5), 584-589.

Lowen, A. (1980). *Fear of life*. New York, New York: Macmillan Publishing Company.

Family and Couples Therapy
in a Time of War

Charles Lee Cole

SUMMARY. In this article the issue of professional responsibility of couples and family therapists is raised with regard to the war in the Persian Gulf. Implications are discussed for families and couples coping with the stress of war and its aftermath.

In late 1990 and the first quarter of 1991, we witnessed our nation's involvement in a major war ranging from the January 15, 1991, deadline to the decision to commit troops to the air campaign and finally the ground campaign that ultimately led to the "victory." During that time the events of the war in the Persian Gulf have caused us all to reflect on our role as marriage and family therapists. What is our responsibility to the families left at home while mothers, fathers, husbands, wives, sons, daughters, grandchildren, nieces, and nephews, etc., have gone to fight a war? Living with the uncertainties of the day-to-day existence of not knowing if their loved ones

Charles Lee Cole, PhD, is Associate Professor of Human Development and Family Studies and Coordinator of the Family Therapy Clinic at Iowa State University. He is a Clinical Member and Approved Supervisor of the American Association for Marriage and Family Therapy, and has a private practice in Ames, IA.

The author would like to express appreciation to Anna L. Cole, MS, who is a Marital and Family Therapist in private practice in Ames, IA, for critically reviewing and making constructive suggestions on this article. The author acknowledges the support of the Department of Human Development and Family Studies and Family and Consumer Sciences Research Institute at Iowa State University for providing support for this project. FCSRI Journal Paper No. 524 of the Family and Consumer Sciences Research Institute, College of Family and Consumer Sciences, Iowa State University, Ames, IA 50011.

are safe and if and when they will return home. As well as what condition they will be in if they do return home. Wondering if they will return unharmed and whole (physically and psychologically) has created a constant state of anxiety for many families in almost every community in our country as well as other countries throughout much of the world as it has in innumerable wars before this one.

REACTIONS TO THE WAR

As most of us have no doubt already discovered, the common reactions of most people were and to some degree continue to be a combination of disbelief that we actually engaged in a major conflict halfway around the globe, a feeling of patriotism and identity with "the cause," remorseful feelings of anguish over the losses of life and opportunities as we watched the "peace dividend" disappear as each bomb dropped and each missile was fired. We knew that the social programs that were to reap the benefits of the "peace dividend" were now being cast into the wind to wither away and possibly die through budgetary reductions that would eliminate them. The war became an almost constant topic of conversation, and people of all ages were faced with questions that they had not had to deal with before. Questions like death and loss that became oh so real for many families where a loved one was killed. The threat of death and loss created anxiety for countless children as well as adults who had fathers, mothers, sons, daughters, uncles, aunts, grandfathers, as well as spouses stationed in the war zone. Some people rallied to action and participated in protests of the war and took a public stand against risking lives in a war conducted for what many perceived as politically and economically motivated reasons. Others took a stand against it on moral grounds, believing that all wars are wrong, and as they marched carried signs with such slogans as "Blood and Oil Don't Mix," "No Lives are Cheap," and "Blood Money, the Cost of Cheap Oil." As these demonstrations went on, other groups held counter demonstrations supporting the president and the decision to go to war and those against the war were labeled unpatriotic. Many people religiously watched the news and became emotionally involved in the war. For some, reports of successes were cheered, and people became wrapped up in the events of the war that they watched unfold during the fighting phase of the war. Sometimes the cheering seemed to be more like that exhibited while watching a sporting event than that appropriate while following the course of a war. When American Patriot Missiles shot down SCUD Missiles aimed at Saudi Arabia or Israel, we felt relief. When the technology did not stop the incoming SCUDS, we felt the anguish of pain experienced by the relatives of those who were killed and injured.

Similarly, we witnessed cheers and the feelings of pride in American technology by many as they heard through briefings how effective our air strikes were and how the "smart bombs" were overwhelmingly succeeding in "knocking out the key targets." The same was heard when General Schwarzkopf briefed the world on the successful ground campaign. This combination of feelings of pride and patriotism by cheering the efforts of the American forces in winning the war was viewed by many as long overdue vindication for what they considered the horrible beating the U.S. had taken in Viet Nam.

These reactions are similar to what some researchers (Jacobs, 1988; Lifton, 1982; Mack, 1984; Macy, 1983; Ptacek, 1988; Rowe, 1985) report regarding families' responses to the threat of nuclear war. The most common response is a tendency to remain in a state of numbness. The reaction of not believing that it is really happening is a part of the initial numbness. Also related is the denial of real threat or danger. Psychologically this may be a functional coping technique at some levels, but it perpetuates a state of helplessness in that people are not prepared for how to deal with the consequences of the immediate and/or potential danger.

The belief that technology will save us by "our good guys outsmarting their bad guys" is a common thread to the desire to have heroes and view our cause as "just and good." The pride that many Americans took in the mastery of our technology as "our 'smart bombs' pinpointed the targets with deadly destruction" suggests that many people have come to believe that "might is right" and that it is easier to deal with enemies by using military power to control them rather than to use diplomatic channels to change the course of history and resolve conflicts. One can only wonder whether this will lead to more use of force, since we were success-ful this time, to quell other storms that threaten the stability of the globe.

This course of events could have far-reaching implications anti-thetical to Satir's (1972) observation (as described in Brothers, 1991) that we lose part of our humanness when we reduce others to objects. By not thinking of the individuals and their uniqueness as members of the planet that we share, we become hardened into not viewing them as valuable human beings. And, when we do that, we lose part of our own humanity and our capacity for being loving, caring people.

As Brothers (1991) points out in her thought-provoking editorial, we live in an interconnected world with instantaneous news and constant communication linkages vis-à-vis satellite transmissions over the airways that flash before us on televisions around the world. In a world of contact through the news and over the tele-phone, we are exposed daily to an expanded circle of influence and given small vignettes of life around the globe. We share the pain and anguish of other human beings as they live in constant fear and mourn relatives who have died in war.

Similarly, we see the faces of Asians, Africans, Russians, Latin Americans, and others on the television and in the newspapers daily and become a little more aware of who they are and what they are concerned about and how they are living, and in this process we develop the potential to become more interdependently cooperative in our common quest to survive and protect the planet that we share.

Modeling for Violence

At another level, it is possible that the modeling of force to resolve conflicts will lead to more violence both within families and within the larger community as groups of individuals (many in gangs) fight each other and catch the rest of us in their crossfire. This increased violence potential creates even more anxiety for families. Many of us will probably or have already seen an increase in violence-related cases in our practices around the country. Cou-ples and families come to us for help in resolving disputes and wanting desperately to find solutions to their problems. It is clear

that for couples and families to achieve intimacy and true connectedness they must learn to respectively deal with differences and
not use and/or abuse power as a means of gaining an advantage over
one's marital partner, children, siblings, and/or parents.

DEALING WITH BOUNDARY AMBIGUITY

Pauline Boss (1980) coined the term "boundary ambiguity" to
describe the anomic condition of having a member of the family
who is psychologically present but physically absent from the family. She originally used this term in her early research on families of
MIA's and POW's during the Viet Nam War (Boss, 1977), but later
applied it to a variety of other contexts. Families where one of their
members is serving in the military in the Persian Gulf certainly have
this occur for them as they try to shift daily routines and responsibilities to take up the slack for the missing member. Wives and husbands whose spouses are stationed in the Persian Gulf have to
assume the duties of their absent marital partners. Children too take
on new roles and adjust to the physical absence by expanding their
range of duties and responsibilities. Both children and the remaining parent assume new rights and privileges that may have belonged
to the missing member. Examples of this would include sitting in a
favorite easy chair, spending time together in carrying out new
rituals and activities that may have formerly been shared with the
missing family member. One case I had involved a woman whose
husband was in the Marines. While her husband was gone, she
began sleeping in the same room as her two young children. When
he comes home, this will require some readjustments that may
become problematic depending upon how long he is gone and how
hard the old patterns are to break. Old patterns established before
the call-up and prolonged absence from family will be difficult for
all parties to reconstruct and reclaim. All members of the family,
both the member in the service and the ones left at home, have
changed during this experience and therefore some of the old patterns that once were meaningful will no longer have the same sa-
lience. In addition, problems that were not solved before the separation will continue and seem to interfere with the happiness the
family feels with the homecoming.

As the missing family members return, they will bring with them a whole set of readjustment issues. In a recent interview with an Air Force pilot that has just been reunited with his family, it became clear that he was experiencing a type of boundary ambiguity too. Part of him was psychologically still back in Saudi Arabia where he had developed his own daily rituals and routines and established close friendships with others sharing the experience with him that he considered to be a surrogate family for him during the last eight months. Figley and Sprenkle (1978) suggest that family therapists need to be attentive to the possible delayed reactions of stress of returning combat veterans. This was certainly evident for returning veterans from the Viet Nam era, and will likely be the case for veterans who returned home after the service in the Persian Gulf War as well. It may be years before evidence of adverse effects emerge–such as the impact on children under two years old of being suddenly separated from military *mothers* as well as fathers.

As we work with these couples and families, we must take into account the indelible changes they have experienced as a result of the separations and help them readjust to each other again. It will be a long painful experience for many and will require the patience and able support of competent marital and family therapists to navigate these uncharted waters.

CONCLUDING COMMENTS

At another level, we must ask ourselves as professionals what our responsibility is to the larger society and to the world at large. Can we and should we play a role in the healing process? Can we and should we be active change agents working to create world peace? As Brothers (1991) points out, Satir clearly felt that to be a professional means being the best human being possible by joining with others to share our connectedness, and thus our capacity for being fully functioning human beings, in making a contribution to making this a better world. One might ask, if not us, then who else has the expertise to take on this vital responsibility that may well have implications for our survival as a planet?

REFERENCES

Boss, P. A. (1977). Clarification of the concept of psychological father presence in families experiencing ambiguity of boundary. *Journal of Marriage and the Family, 39,* 141-151.

Boss, P. A. (1980). Normative family stress: Family boundary changes across the life-span. *Family Relations, 29,* 445-450.

Brothers, B. J. (1991). Ask not for whom the siren wails. *Journal of Couples Therapy, 2,* 1-5.

Figley, C. R. & Sprenkel, D. H. (1978). Delayed stress response syndrome: Family therapy implications. *Journal of Marriage and Family Counseling, 4,* 53-60.

Jacobs, J. B. (1988). Families facing the nuclear taboo. *Family Relations 37,* 432-436.

Lifton, R. J. (1982). Beyond psychic numbing: A call to awareness. *American Journal of Orthopsychiatry, 53,* 619-629.

Mack, J. E. (1984). Resistance to knowing in the nuclear age. *Harvard Educational Review, 54,* 260-270.

Macy, J. R. (1983). *Despair and personal power in the nuclear age.* Philadelphia: New Society Publishers.

Ptacek, C. (1988). The nuclear age: Context for family interaction. *Family Relations, 37,* 437-443.

Rowe, D. (1985). *Living with the bomb: Can we live without enemies?* Boston: Routledge and Kegan Paul.

Satir, V. (1972). *Peoplemaking,* Palo Alto, CA: Science and Behavior.